Comments on *The Contras*

Would that I alone could effect a wide distribution of a particular book...this book would be my choice. I found the interviews fascinating, horrifying, and faithful to all reports I've gotten from other witnesses. *The Contras: Interviews with Anti-Sandinistas* could change the course of our foreign policy in Nicaragua.

Edward Asner

This book is an unusual addition to the growing shelf of new volumes on Central America, for the voices we hear in it are those of the contras now waging war against the government of Nicaragua. They talk with astonishing frankness about their training and experience in torture and assassination. Because most of them still apparently believe in their cause, their testimony constitutes an irrefutable indictment of what Reagan is doing in Central America. These are unashamed terrorists who are being trained and supplied with U.S. tax dollars.

Adam Hochschild,
Mother Jones

A startling document! A candid self-analysis by the people President Reagan calls "the moral equal of our founding fathers...." A *must* for any American citizen who cares about the truth, this country, or the future.

Mike Farrell

(more)

These interviews are a stunning corrective to the Reagan administration's overblown rhetoric about "freedom fighters" and "founding fathers."

Victor Perera,
journalist and author of
The Last Lords of Palenque

The most comprehensive documentation of the origin, make-up, and insanely brutal purpose of the contras from the contras themselves. Finally a true picture of Mr. Reagan's favorite terrorists.

Martin Sheen

Read these interviews and decide for yourself if these lost souls (rapists, thieves, murderers, the unloved, captive peasants, and frightened children) deserve to receive your tax dollars—in the form of any kind of aid—to continue their vile, bloody, and utterly doomed work against the people and the earth of Nicaragua. These men *are* death. With U.S. assistance, our money, they can only buy more of themselves.

Alice Walker

The contras exist as an extension of U.S. interventionism in the Third World. Subsidized and supplied by the Reagan administration for years, they now enjoy the approval of the U.S. Congress.

This book further documents that U.S. taxpayer dollars subsidize murder, rape, pillage, and the destruction of Nicaragua's economy. This book will make you want to weep for the victimized people in Nicaragua and angry enough to challenge U.S. policies in Central America.

Congressman Ronald V. Dellums
U.S. House of Representatives,
California

THE CONTRAS
Interviews with Anti-Sandinistas

THE CONTRAS
Interviews with Anti-Sandinistas

Dieter Eich and Carlos Rincón

Synthesis Publications San Francisco

Cover: Vanda Sendzimir
Photos: Murry Sill and William F. Gentile

Copyright 1984 by Konkret Literatur Verlag, Hamburg,
Federal Republic of Germany

English translation Copyright © 1985 Synthesis Publications
All English language rights reserved. No portion of this book may be
reproduced, by any process or technique, without the express written
consent of the publisher.

Library of Congress Cataloging in Publication Data

Main entry under title:

The Contras: interviews with anti-Sandinistas

  Translation of: La contra.
  1. Nicaragua—Politics and government—1979 -
2. Counterrevolutions—Nicaragua.   3. Interviews—Nicaragua.
I. Eich, Dieter.   II. Rincón, Carlos.
F1528.C66413   1985   972.85'053   85-14844
ISBN 0-89935-051-8

Published by Synthesis Publications
2703 Folsom Street, San Francisco, CA 94110

Printed in the United States of America
10 9 8 7 6 5 4 3 2 1

Acknowledgments

To the translators, for their excellent and rapidly completed work. They are: Margot Brunner, Jamie Owen Daniel, Dr. Joseph Hahn, Renny Harrigan, Mary S. Lederer, and Cathy Neff.

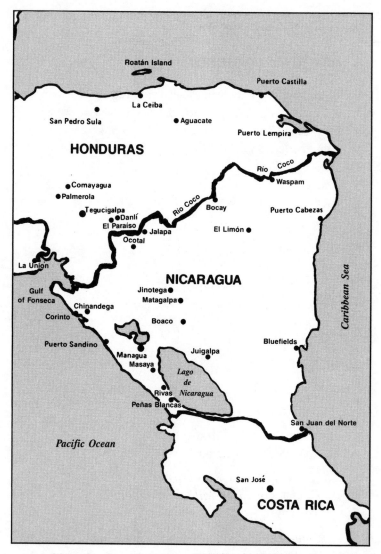

Map showing places to which the interviews refer.

Contents

Foreword
to the U.S. Edition

The Contras provides an oral history of the covert actions against Nicaragua, the most public secret war, which has caused more controversy in the United States than any episode since the Vietnam War. The book is a self-portrait: the contras speak for themselves, in their own words. They express their reality as they see it through their individual histories and goals.

The authors often found themselves in odd places in the course of ferreting out the individual stories behind the contra war. The dark but tidy cafeteria tucked away in a prosperous bank building on the main avenue of San José, Costa Rica, was a far cry from Rick's Cafe in Casablanca. Not so the small roadside motel, where rooms were more often than not rented by the hour—a prototype of the desperado's hangout—in Danlí, a small Honduran town 20 miles from the Nicaraguan border. And so it went, the contacts in smoke-filled bars, in immaculate lawyers' offices, in the moody corners of dim restaurants, in hotel rooms by prearranged signals. And these contacts were only the beginning. The labyrinth more often than not led to secret safe houses, although some of them, like the covert war itself, were not so secret. In one interview, a knock on the wrong door of a quiet residential street in Tegucigalpa, Honduras, brought a friendly answer from the owner, who simply pointed out that the safe house in question was five houses down the road.

In all of these cases, as well as in interviews held with prisoners in jails located throughout Nicaragua and with wounded contras in Managua and Honduras, our methodology followed a consistent pattern. We told our subjects that we wished to talk to them about their personal histories: the who, where, what, why, and how of their involvement in "the contra" and subsequent activities. We wanted to know how these men thought and felt, how they saw their involvement with "the contra," what motivated them. We asked each person to present his personal point of view, his own perceptions of the contra organization with which he was or had been involved.

No one except the authors and their subjects were present during these extensive conversations. The interviews were taped with the knowledge and consent of the subjects, who could say when they wanted the tape-recorder stopped for an off-the-record comment.

In this fashion 95 individuals were interviewed, producing a total of 340 hours of taped material. The facts contained in the interviews and reports presented in this book have been confirmed independently with at least two other, separate sources. This system of corroboration forced us to discard interviews, despite the interesting material some of them contained. Examples are an interview with one of the first Nicaraguan Democratic Force (FDN) comandantes to use the CIA manual, another with a two-time deserter who dedicated himself to rustling cattle from Nicaragua at ARDE's expense, and yet another with a Moravian priest who was also a MISURA collaborator. Despite their intrinsic interest, these interviews had to be set aside because the facts contained in them could not be confirmed. Indeed, some of the testimony appeared to be deliberately falsified. Thus, each interview in this book has been chosen according to somewhat paradoxical criteria: whether it realistically portrays the situation in subjective terms and is in fact a self-portrayal, and whether the self-revelation presents an objective reality, a reality that reveals and reconstitutes the development of the contras from inside, through oral history.

In the interviews, we follow the defeat and dismantling of dictator Anastasio Somoza's National Guard to the activities of scattered armed bands and diverse small terrorist groups (to use the language of a U.S. congressional document about the pre-FDN Legion of September 15th) and finally to the present organization of regional commands. Portrayed here are the very first safe houses, the training camps in the United States and along the Honduran border with Nicaragua. From a rag-tag collection of former Guardsmen, the group begins to take shape with the first infusion of international financing in 1980. Miskito rebel groups start to form, and in Costa Rica, ARDE—which appeared to enjoy the most support at that time—also begins to take shape. The situation changes dramatically when the Reagan administration, apparently on the advice of the Central Intelligence Agency, decides to unite the distinct groups under the hegemony of the FDN, dominated by former National Guardsmen. $19 million makes this decision a reality: a group of 500 paramilitary men, the cornerstone of the true beginning of the covert war in December 1981.

The contras tell their own stories. Edén Pastora, the would-be international revolutionary who failed at being the supreme leader of the Central American guerrilla movement, breathes life into ARDE on Nicaragua's southern border. Task Forces for which there are no off-limits begin to form on the northern border. The war intensifies. One thing is clear: while the Reagan administration may have seen aid to the contra movement as a way of stopping arms shipments along the "Ho Chi Minh Trail" from Nicaragua to El Salvador, the contras have always seen their goal as bringing down the government in Managua. President Reagan said it in his own words in a February 21, 1985, press conference: make the Sandinistas say "Uncle."

In this book, in their own words, the contras tell the story behind this goal, and how a disheveled, motley crew of would-be soldiers grew into a force of 15,000 or more men. They give valuable, informative insights, which have scientific merit, as to why covert action—a specter of the 1960s past that failed—continues to motivate U.S. policy toward Nicaragua today.

Dieter Eich and Carlos Rincón
July 21, 1985

"Honor Prevented Us From Serving the New Regime"

Conversation with Isaías Cuadra Espinoza

I was born in 1933 in the proud city of Masaya. Even as a small boy, I was interested in the military. I therefore entered the Nicaraguan Military Academy in 1949, and graduated successfully in 1953. I improved my knowledge by going to study in other countries, several times, and I specialized in police work.

Where did you take this specialized course?

In Peru. In the National Academy of the Civil Guard. I have nothing but very good and unforgettable memories of that time in school. I am grateful for it; it was an important part of my education as an officer. Today I must admit that I should have been able to achieve more on the basis of that education. I could have performed my work better. But what's the use of such regrets. My conscience is clear, because I was an honest and exemplary policeman. Being a police officer is a profession in which one is subjected to the widest variety of influences, to all facets of human life—a job that is extraordinarily difficult and carries great responsibility.

How long did you train in Peru?

This special training lasted four years.

After that, where did you work in Nicaragua?

I immediately joined the police force in Managua, in the National Security command. I successfully carried out my duties there and later assumed command of the Guard Battalion of His Excellency, the General of the Battalion and President of the Republic, Anastasio Somoza. I was also in charge of the model prison here, where I now sit as a prisoner. Shortly before the government of General Somoza came to an end, I was retired. At that point I was a Colonel. The entire National Guard was placed under the command of a new General Staff.

What did you do in June of 1979?

In June of 1979 I was in charge of the First Battalion, the Guard Battalion. The Battalion was made up of the best soldiers and officers. Many were graduates of the School of Basic Training (Escuela de Entrenamiento Básico, EEBI). Serving in the First Battalion was considered a great honor, as was serving in any other branch of the National Guard. Except that in our battalion, the people had been especially chosen because we were directly responsible for the safety of the President of the Republic.

Let's talk about July, 1979. What happened during that month?

The General Staff made some important decisions during this period. I could take part only indirectly in the discussions and decision-making, which were carried out by the highest officers in the country. One result of the discussions affected all of the older officers in the National Guard.

We were supposed to be retired, in order to open up the higher ranks to younger men. I no longer remember clearly whether these negotiations were part of a particular agreement that had been reached with the special ambassador from the United States. I also no longer remember who took part in them. The result, in any case, was that officers who were advanced in age were supposed to be retired.

Were new demands placed on the National Guard? Was it a question of finally bringing the guerrilla war to an end?

Almost all of the officers' corps of the National Guard had been trained in counterinsurgency at a wide variety of training camps in the United States, the Panama Canal Zone, and South America. So that could not have been the reason. In retrospect, I assume that they wanted to replace those officers who were too closely connected to the government of General Somoza. With the re-structuring of the General Staff, a new element also entered into the command structure—these promotions were meant to bring the National Guard into line.

How did you feel when you realized that one of the main results of the negotiations was your retirement?

It was a very hard blow. But let me go back a step. I am a colonel and had the opportunity, within that rank, to extend my command authority. My next promotion would have been to the rank of major. Under the new arrangement, it was no longer possible for me to be promoted. But all of the officers with the same sort of training and of the same age group accepted this decision with discipline, and retired without protest. For us, the only question was how we would adjust to civilian life.

With respect to these negotiations, didn't you feel as if you were being led around by the nose? It was in fact quite clear that they intended to leave you out in the cold.

No, I wouldn't put it that way. We all felt that this was a sacrifice which had to be asked of us. We were released from the officers' corps so that peace and harmony could again prevail. We accepted this decision like the disciplined soldiers we had been throughout our military careers. We believed that by doing so, we would contribute to the national harmony which was needed just then, and for which we had all been waiting.

What did you do after you had been retired?

I lived in the military colony located on the mountain right behind the Hotel Intercontinental. I was allowed to continue living there until I found a new house. At the same time, I was able to continue to visit the First Battalion, with which I felt very close ties. In turning over my command authority to the new officers, I wanted to stay on the sidelines in an advisory capacity. The command of this battalion was taken on by a lieutenant-colonel. Nothing of particular importance happened until July 18, 1979. On the 19th I received information to the effect that the General Staff was no longer to be found at headquarters. There was no longer anyone there who could assume command.

Which military personnel left the country on July 17?

I don't know. I didn't see them when they left the Presidential Palace or boarded the plane. I also don't know who accompanied His Excellency on the plane. When I then heard that the General Staff had left the country, there was nothing left to do. There was supposed to be a Red Cross gathering point at the Air Force barracks, where all officers could entrust themselves to the protection of this international organization. We were supposed to bring our families there as well.

Did you go to the Red Cross gathering point?

Yes. We went over to the Air Force barracks; I led a group of soldiers, who all turned in their weapons there. The Red Cross took down information on us and prepared lists, asking which of us wanted to be deported to El Salvador, Honduras, Guatemala, or to any other country. The Red Cross had promised the General Staff to get anyone seeking protection out of the country, together with their families. There were a great many family members, civilian personnel, and children of close relatives who wanted to leave.

That same day, everyone who had come to the gathering point was brought to the Zona Franca, because they couldn't stay in the Air Force barracks. We remained in the Zona Franca under the protection of the Red Cross until July 24. That day, we were informed that all of the men were to be brought together on a particular stretch of land, and the women and children were to be relocated to other shelters. This made it clear to us that our situation had worsened dramatically. On the next day, what we had feared came to pass. All of the men were taken from the Zona Franca to the model prison, imprisoned, and turned over to the new authorities.

Why didn't you flee the country before this? Or did you want to seek asylum in a different way?

Officers have a moral duty to stay with their soldiers. Without leadership they totally lose their heads, and for me there was no alternative but to face the new situation with them.

What did you think of the officers who had fled?

I didn't think about them. They were gone, following the motto: save yourself if you can. But it was too late for me to criticize the reasons why we had been left without leadership.

Does your family still live in Managua?

No, I arranged for my family to flee to a particular embassy and from there they received free passage.

When did you realize that a great number of the National Guard had deserted?

There are situations in a person's life when you have to decide to seek asylum or to get on a plane and leave the country. Both are decisions that people make in a critical situation from which they want to escape somehow. I am not aware that anyone has criticized the behavior of those who left the country. On the contrary, we felt relieved that some had been lucky enough to escape.

An old comrade-in-arms of yours, the former commander of Ocotal, said when he learned that Somoza had left the country: "I consider the behavior of His Excellency to be treason, desertion."

I don't share that view. Nor what might be said about the General Staff and the other officers who left Nicaragua.

When were you sure that the National Guard no longer existed, had disbanded?

On the day that General Somoza left, I had the impression that everything had come to an end, that we had reached a point where there was no longer any chance of negotiating. Those who were in power or, to put it in a better way, those who had the weapons were not prepared to share their command authority with the remainder of the National Guard. It was a hopeless situation; we no longer mixed, we couldn't even breathe the same air. It was clear that, as far as the new people in power were concerned, we could not be trusted. For this reason, everything had come to an end.

Why, in your opinion, was the integration of former National Guard personnel into the new military not possible? We know that the United States in particular had insisted on the existence of this possibility during negotiations.

It was impossible. First of all, we are separated by ideology, and then there is the matter of military honor, which prohibits such integration. The idea that anyone could come to such an agreement seems impossible to me. We had a certain ideology and were disarmed because of our ideals. Honor absolutely prevented us from serving the new regime. Let me explain this in greater detail. We served a particular government, whose elected president was Division General Somoza. But this did not mean for a moment that we were a political army.

Interestingly, the military make-up of the National Guard differs greatly from the usual military structures in Latin America— particularly because of the direct ties that the Guard had with the Somoza dynasty, serving as the backbone of its domination. And this coincided with the general strategy of the United States. It's not unimportant that the National Guard was founded at the request of the U.S.

I can't agree with that. Within its guidelines, the National

Guard is a non-political institution. What confused most people, or what they misunderstood, is the fact that the National Guard is closely tied to the presidency. For a long time, the elected presidents bore the name Somoza. Anyone who is trying to degrade a particular institution will look for—or construct—every conceivable fact to strengthen his hypothesis. There are definitely some people who explain the whole situation from their own perspective, but I can confirm the fact that all of the officers, the entire National Guard, were proud of their service and fulfilled their duties conscientiously. We served our fatherland, although some people say that we served the interests of the Somoza family and not those of the fatherland. That is the problem.

How long did you actually work in the National Security administration? Surely this institution was greatly feared.

I was in the Office of National Security from 1956 to 1976. Twenty years altogether. I never looked upon my job as anything special, it was a purely administrative job.

How was it possible that the archives of the state security service were not destroyed before the victory of the FSLN, with the result that they fell into the hands of the enemy intact?

I don't know anything about that. At the time I was no longer in that office. It had already been two years since I had seen service there for the last time. But it was really irresponsible that they were not destroyed.

Doesn't it indicate the chaos that existed everywhere? Surely it would have been possible to destroy a portion of the secret archives and leave another portion with incorrect data, so as to provoke mistrust and suspicion within the FSLN.

What's the point of talking about it now? The state archives remained intact; such ideas are useless. That's enough!

How did you experience the insurrection?

Today, five years after the fact, everybody has an answer,

everyone knows what could have been done better. I don't see any point in thinking about it. But when you set aside all the factors that provoked such a change, the answer is clear. The National Guard was no longer in a position to put down the insurrection. It was no longer getting any help. We had been left in the lurch by the rest of the world at this point, with the exception of a small number of countries.

Didn't you have any more weapons?

We no longer had any weapons, and economically there were a great many limitations. As far back as 1977 or, more correctly 1976, they began to decrease our funds. The general supply for the army was reduced, training was cut back; everyone suffered from the shortage of supplies. In order to be sure of good production—no matter where, in the army or in other branches of society—it is extremely important to have at your disposal good human materiel that is constantly replenished. We had grown old, and it was better to have new elements take over our positions of leadership. It was no longer possible for us to set up our own training camps, because we are a developing country which doesn't have the resources for this at its disposal. We don't possess any technology and we also don't have the necessary materials. Without generous assistance and financing from outside, everything has to collapse.

What other factors played a role in the situation?

I could include other factors, of course, but they would be political. For this reason I am not interested in discussing them. As a soldier, I can simply tell you that there were no clear-cut mistakes that explain the failure. There was battle fatigue, which affected all personnel. Our personnel had been severely reduced; the army didn't have the quantity of combat troops needed to successfully overcome the profusion of problems it faced. We repeatedly had to pull personnel from one location and transfer them to another. The wear and tear which results from this sort of thing is extraordinarily great. We were able to secure certain positions adequately, and thereby lost entire cities. This is what drained the National Guard.

Then you don't see the defeat as having resulted from erroneous military decisions?

The reasons for the defeat were political. Politics prevented us from receiving the necessary support—the materiel we needed, munitions, adequate weapons—so that we could operate in a manner appropriate to the military situation.

Don't you believe that during the period we are talking about, the years 1978 and 1979, political conditions inside Nicaragua were a decisive factor in the insurrection?

If it is possible for someone to be defeated militarily, it is because he has made a lot of military errors and abandoned military principles. Today we can say that several of our military principles were no longer successful. But the spirit that moves individuals to hold out until the very end needs logistical support in order to adapt to given situations. It is, however, clear that there was initially very little support for the Sandinista movement and that it only grew over the course of time.

How do you explain this? Don't you think that it was extraordinarily important to the outcome of this revolution that the great majority of the population was against the National Guard?

No, that was not the most important thing. It was the invasion from outside the country that was responsible. There was an invasion of mercenaries, or, as they are called today, internationalists from all countries, who supported the Sandinista Front. In contrast, the National Guard was worn down and had grown weary from many skirmishes; it no longer had enough strength to deal with the whole problem without outside help.

We have noticed that even in prison you still adhere to military rank.

That is only a symbol of mutual respect. But in reality we are all prisoners. I was sentenced by a court to 30 years and that's the end of that.

Do you believe you were justly sentenced?

I don't know what you are getting at with that question.

How does it feel to be captive in the prison of which you were once the director?

Nothing special. This is the way the cards are dealt in life. Today I exist and tomorrow I don't. Therefore it makes no sense to look back and blubber about it all. If I thought about what I might have done differently, I would probably drive myself crazy. As I have already told you, I was dealt a bad hand and so there is no point in looking back. Of course I would like to do something else, but that's not possible. I am locked up here unjustly, like all of the others who are imprisoned here. So I am not embittered and I am not driving myself crazy, thinking about whether the life I led before was good or bad. I only know that the life I led at that time had some masochistic aspects to it.

But everyone repeatedly comes to grips with his past . . .

Of course it is very interesting to reflect back on the past. But we don't discuss such things with the others who are here in jail now. We try to pass the time as best we can and to make no more problems for ourselves than are absolutely necessary. Of course I could tell you how it feels to be here in prison, looking for a ray of hope in all this darkness. But that would only be a burden, and tiresome—it would just make things even more confusing.

Plan C and Operation M83

Here the authors present background information to a number of the interviews that follow. The names of persons who are interviewed in this book have been italicized; they include several high-ranking figures among the contras. Most of the information concerns two strategies initiated by the CIA for the contras: Plan C of 1982-83, which failed, and its successor, Operation "M83."

On January 27, 1982, the ex-lieutenant of the EEBI, *Jorge Ignacio Ramírez Zelaya*, arrives from Buenos Aires at the airport in Tegucigalpa. He is traveling with an Argentine passport. His later admission as an assistant to the FDN General Staff is only the beginning of his steady rise. His organizational abilities make him indispensable when the Las Vegas training camp and others are set up on Honduran territory. In preparing the camps, he works closely with troop leaders *Armando López, "El Policía,"* and *Pedro Pablo Ortiz Centeno, "El Suicida."* He also becomes one of the organizers of the first FDN training camps for Miskitos. His code name as an officer is "B1." He and *Pedro Javier Núñez Cabezas*, later a secret service officer, belong to the FDN officer corps that is responsible for carrying out—and then takes over the leadership of—Operation M83.

The first strategy that CIA specialists worked out for the FDN General Staff was Plan C. This plan called for masses of FDN troops to swarm into Nicaragua from camps in Honduras. The goal was to establish a "liberated territory" and to destroy the coffee harvest in the Matagalpa and Jinotega districts. According to the testimony of CIA officials before the U.S. Congress, this meant that daily planning and coordination of actions by the FDN forces and the CIA were already taking place in February 1983. Núñez Cabezas, secret service chief to "El Suicida," had received special training in an intensive course in Buenos Aires.

"El Suicida" participated in repeated operations designed to take the small border town of Jalapa. On January 8, 1983, he ordered María and Felipe Barreda to be shot through the head [by Núñez]. The couple had traveled to the northern border of Nicaragua to take part in the coffee harvest as volunteers. Before being murdered, they were dragged by "El Suicida's" people to Honduras, where they were interrogated. The Barredas were supposed to be forced to give testimony in favor of the FDN, and a team from the "September 15th" Radio Station was supposed to record this testimony. The interrogators, however, could not force the Barredas to give up their position of support for the Sandinistas.

Plan C also called for the civilian population to be drawn into the fight. Villages and state cooperatives in the immediate area were attacked and seized. On March 26, 1983, the tiny village of Rancho Grande was hit by a mortar attack under the command of "Renato." The French doctor Pierre Grosjean died along with other civilians.

* * *

"Zompopo" is the name of a red, leaf-eating ant. It is from this ant that a strip of land not far from Matagalpa derives its name. In the Zompopera region, during the months of March and April, 1983, the contras set up road blocks to stop private and government vehicles. On April 30, 1983, a car occupied by Albrecht Pflaum of the West German Development Agency (DED), three nurses, and a bank official falls into one of these traps. They are shot dead by the side of the road, by *Eduardo López Valenzuela* and others.

* * *

After the unsuccessful attempt of the contras to take Jalapa and Teotecacinte [a small border village] under Plan C, a phase of massive infiltration began: Operation M83. Operation M83 had various goals. Supply and communication lines to the Sandinista army were to be cut off, the FSLN was to suffer political blows, and the population was to be demoralized by terrorist attacks on important public figures. The Sandinista army answered with a change in tactics. It no longer attempted to stop contra fighting units right at the border; instead it let them penetrate far into the country where they would be cut off from supplies of weapons, food, and clothing, and isolated.

When Ramírez Zelaya of the FDN General Staff was made responsible for Operation M83, he expressly requested from his superiors the collaboration of the young secret service officer Núñez Cabezas, whom he had met during his short stay in "El Suicida's" camp. After a short, special course in the use of explosives, both went to Nicaragua secretly on May 29, 1983. Núñez Cabezas goes by the name of "El Muerto." His two older brothers are also called that.

* * *

The C47 military plane—camouflage-colored, without any national identification number—rolls off the runway at "El Agua-cate" Airport in the Honduran department of Olacho on October 3, 1983, as it has done before. It is piloted by *Roberto Amador Narváez*. He was a major in the Nicaraguan air force and is now second commanding officer of the FDN air-strike forces. The co-pilot is ex-Captain Hugo Aguilar. Together, the two pilots have 16,000 hours of flight experience. The crew is at the level of the U.S. Air Force in terms of parachuting and dropping supplies. The flight plan on this day calls for deep penetration of Nicaraguan territory in order to drop 15,000 pounds of supplies in eight bundles. The supplies are for the combat units commanded by "Renato" in Matagalpa province.

The plane, flying at a considerable altitude, crosses the border not far from the Las Vegas base and establishes radio contact with the unit, to prepare for the drop. But the drop never takes place. The plane is hit by anti-aircraft fire from Sandinista border troops; one engine catches fire and the pilots are forced to make an emergency landing. Including this C47, the FDN loses nine airplanes and helicopters in Nicaragua.

In August 1984, another C47 follows, piloted by ex-Major José Luis Gutiérrez (formerly the pilot for Somoza's son "El Chiguín"), along with a UH-500-D helicopter, armed with an MG and twelve rockets.

* * *

Emerson Uriel Navarrete, "El Judío," a former agent in the Somozan secret service and an active member of the FDN, had participated not only in various border raids but also in "Operación Agrícola." This operation called for the recruitment of peasants into the FDN, and for the sabotage of agricultural production centers in the Chinandega region. "El Judío" was selected by the FDN General Staff to take a course in marine sabotage, taught by North American instructors, on the Honduran island of Roatán. This special training for FDN personnel was intensified in conjunction with plans to destroy the oil tanks at the harbor at Corinto and the oil pipelines at Puerto Sandino, and with plans to mine Nicaragua's harbors. In April 1984, the mining of the harbors from American mother-ships under the direction of the CIA met with disapproval from Americans and also from allies of the U.S.

* * *

1960 was, for two reasons, a decisive year in the history of the Miskito communities. First, the decision of the International Court went into effect, giving the left bank of the Río Coco to Honduras. The Río Coco became a border river. Second, the last North American banana company discontinued production on the Atlantic Coast; exploitation of the giant pine forests began. A whole group of Indian communities was to be robbed of its land. The Indians were placed in a large resettlement complex, so that they could not cause any problems for the big lumber companies. The complex was called "Tasba raya" and consisted of five settlements. One of these, founded in 1972 with approximately 5,000 inhabitants, was Francia Sirpe.

In 1982, the Miskitos from four of the settlements were displaced to Honduras. It was to be expected that the same thing would happen to Francia Sirpe and indeed it did, at the end of the year. The fact that Bishop Salvador Schlaefer was among the deported inhabitants brought this event, which included a long march on foot, to the attention of the media. *Orlando Wayland*, Miskito, relates what happened in detail.

"My Assignment Was Just to Blow Up the Cement Factory"

Conversation with William Baltodano Herrera

My name is William Baltodano Herrera. I was born in 1953, and I live in Diriamba.

What did you study?

I studied construction engineering.

Were you politically active as a student?

When I began studying at the university, it became clear to me that it was urgent for us to fight for radical political change in our country. You know, of course, that the Somoza regime was one of the bloodiest and most brutal in Latin America. This fanatical dictatorship enraged almost the entire population, and challenged the people to fight it. Every politically concerned citizen felt called upon to take part in this struggle. I was active in the FSLN and was responsible for one whole region.

Which region?

The southern region, the Carazo and Rivas districts. We were under the leadership of Comandante Oscar Pérez Casar and Comandante Jaime Wheelock. I know both of them very well. I organized the students, and after that I concentrated on the general mobilization that was beginning throughout the country, and on weapons transport. These were tasks I could carry out with no problem. Later I was responsible for transporting the weapons of the FSLN from Costa Rica to Nicaragua. My most spectacular feat was hitting Somoza's bunker from the Hotel Intercontinental with a rocket.

Together with "Negro" Chamorro?

Yes, exactly, with "Negro" [Fernando] Chamorro, in collaboration with the FSLN.

Can you tell us something about working with Chamorro?

At that time, the September 11th revolutionary movement headed by Chamorro wanted to join with the Frente Sandinista. But because of political and strategic differences, this never occurred. "Negro" Chamorro then decided to launch an action with his group, on its own. The action was supposed to demonstrate that the Somoza forces could be hit, accurately, even in the middle of Managua. The attack against the EEBI was an example of that. It was coordinated by the Chamorro brothers, "Negro" and Edmundo. Emed Lang and Oscar Casar Pérez [sic] were also there. I myself brought the 12 rockets we wanted to use for the attack from a safe house in Masaya to Managua, by jeep. We then mounted two of the rockets on the top floor of the Hotel Intercontinental. I laid out the complete electrical system for firing them. I had taken a couple of special courses in that, so I could handle the stuff well, and also deal with explosives.

Did you carry out any other actions in the struggle against Somoza?

The FSLN had commissioned me to recruit about 300 youths who wanted to take up arms against Somoza. I did that in two and a half days. With this group we captured Carazo and the city of Diriamba. That was on the 10th and the 12th of September, 1978. We only had 16 rapid-fire machine guns, but we constantly battled the National Guard anyway.

Then I had to leave the country because I had received a couple of superficial gunshot wounds. The FSLN wanted me to go to Costa Rica to take over an important new assignment. At this time the military command was coordinated from Costa Rica. I went to La Cruz in Costa Rica via Sapoa. We were immediately arrested there by the Civil Guards. We stayed in prison for a while. The Frente assigned me to the southern front, which was under the command of Edén Pastora.

At that time there were still problems between the Frente Sandinista and the September 11th movement, that is, problems between "Negro" Chamorro and Edén Pastora. I think there were differences over military leadership. Chamorro is a very individualistic type.

What do you mean by individualistic?

"El Negro" is an individualist; he wants to do everything *he* thinks is correct. But in the difficult situation that existed, it was impossible for everyone to do whatever popped into his head. This very often led to arguments.

Shortly before the uprising [the final stage of the struggle against Somoza], I had a difficult personal problem. My daughter became very sick. At that time my family was already living in Costa Rica. The child had a heart disease and desperately needed an operation. I had to take care of her and couldn't participate in the uprising. I returned to Nicaragua six months after the victory. My daughter's recovery had gone very slowly. A lot of people didn't understand that. But when we set out to fight for the rights of the people, we also have to protect and defend our families. Our families are, after all, part of the people.

You returned, then, at the end of 1979?

We returned to Nicaragua on December 30, 1979. To this day, I can't understand why my old comrades-in-arms treated me so badly after I returned. Naturally I kept in touch with Chamorro and [Vizente] Rappaciolli the whole time.

"Negro" Chamorro also came to Nicaragua and worked with the Frente Sandinista up to a certain point. When he was no longer in agreement with certain things, he returned to private life. His brother Edmundo remained in Costa Rica. In any case, we lost contact because I was busy with my family the whole time. But when I wanted to rejoin the Frente Sandinista, I was simply given the brush-off.

Why do you think you were no longer accepted?

To many, I had become something like a renegade. I asked the Frente to give me new assignments. I didn't have to excuse myself because I didn't fight in that important phase (the uprising). My reason was clear. But now I wanted to fight with them again. I also needed work in order to survive in this critical situation.

As an engineer, which is one of the most respected professions in Nicaragua, you must certainly have been able to find work.

That's what I thought, too. I looked everywhere for work, but all the doors remained closed to me. That hurt me personally. I believe that the decision to take up arms against my former comrades was already lurking in my subconscious. After that, everything went pretty quickly. I joined the counterrevolution because I was practically suffocating from rejection. I was completely isolated. For me, there was no longer any future in Nicaragua. I was pressured on all sides, especially by the political base of the Frente, not as much by the political leadership. A lot of people were against me for personal reasons. That was especially insulting and completely narrowed my horizons. The counterrevolution took advantage of my bad situation. I once explained my position to Vizente Rappaciolli. His answer was short and clear: the best thing for me would be to join the armed opposition abroad.

When was that?

Around April, 1981. At that time I had a job as a work-gang leader in a tree-cutting brigade. We cleared out old coffee plantations. I earned 3,000 córdobas doing that. One can't support a family on that. My professional qualifications no longer had anything to do with it. Because I was desperate, I took any job.

Could your problems also have been connected to the fact that you had close links with Chamorro and Rappaciolli, which the Frente didn't like?

There were a lot of problems that came together. Certainly one can include this connection. I still remember that my first question to Vizente Rappaciolli was how he assessed the possibility of the counterrevolution winning in Nicaragua. Rappaciolli believed it wasn't the time for deep analysis. The Sandinistas were clearly moving in the direction of Marxism-Leninism. My connections with the Chamorro brothers, who were already in charge of the counterrevolutionary movement UDN, would soon bring me to ruin. UDN was the political organization, and the FARN its military arm. Then I joined the UDN-FARN.

Were you also convinced that Nicaragua was already being governed along Marxist-Leninist lines? What did that mean to you?

I have never been afraid of Marxism-Leninism. Up to a certain point, it's a progressive movement. I have read the classics of Marxism-Leninism and become informed about Marxist-Leninist political leaders. No, I've never been afraid of it. I didn't join the contras for this reason; rather, I was deeply insulted by the rejection of me as a person. I think that was the real reason.

What did it mean to become active in the FARN? What assignments did you have to undertake?

It was completely clear to them that I was good with weapons. Some of them had even taken courses I once taught. They saw in me a new, important pillar of strength for the new structure of the organization. I was to take on an important function in the military structure, immediately.

What military function were you to assume?

When I joined the UDN-FARN, the armed branch was just being built up. I was supposed to take the third position in the military hierarchy.

What political program did the FARN begin with?

The political structure was developed by people whose political past in Nicaragua was flawless. They were anti-Somoza. At that time, no one thought of building the core of a new political movement with people who had had ties to the overthrown regime. No one would have supported such a movement. A structure had to be built that was supported by people with a clean political past —a difficult undertaking in those times. We were building the administrative staff and the general directorate. Edmundo Chamorro headed it. Cabo Centeno and a couple of other men with a great deal of political experience belonged to it. The idea was that no one would be in a position *politically* to really threaten the Frente Sandinista. Therefore it was absolutely necessary to become *militarily* active as quickly as possible. The people had to see that our stand was not just gibberish, but that we were becoming a military power in Nicaragua. That's how the idea of the Internal Front was born.

"Negro" Chamorro was still in Nicaragua at the time. We summoned him to Costa Rica. He was supposed to abandon everything in Nicaragua because the time was ripe for action. And then "Negro" Chamorro, Juan Zavala, and a couple of other important political personages came to Costa Rica.

Did the gold-smuggling that people attribute to Juan Zavala really make possible the financing of the UDN-FARN?

I am not informed about that.

But if one builds up such an organization and has an important function in it, he must certainly know how the financing is arranged.

I already told you I have no information about that.

What position did you take?

The Comandante-en-Jefe [Commander-in-Chief] was "Negro" Chamorro. Juan Zavala followed him. I was in third place in the military organization. In August, we travelled abroad to make our political ideas known. First we went to Argentina and Venezuela.

Were you also looking for advisers?

No, we were only looking for people with money.

In Buenos Aires you were received by General Balín...

You certainly are familiar with the story. We stayed in Argentina for three days. General Balín, who was at that time Chief of the General Staff, received us along with Captain Davido. We explained our program to both of them in detail. The Chamorros were in charge of the political part. The important contacts with the Argentine and American governments went through them. Bolaños was in charge of the international relations of the organization. I handled the military part. If the discussion touched upon military questions, I represented the FARN.

What interest did the Argentines have in building a well-trained military unit in a foreign country? Did they want to give only military advice or also political guidance?

As I said, I was only concerned with the military part. They showed great interest in that area. Beyond that, of course they were interested in our politics and how we intended to bring our political ideas into the heart of Nicaragua. We arranged for the Argentines to send military advisers to us in Costa Rica and Tegucigalpa. This way they could also control how their money was being spent. The Argentines treated us well. We were practically official guests. The government took charge of everything; we were driven everywhere, invited out everywhere, and we didn't have to pay for anything.

Did you also get a special entry visa?

No, of course not. We came in as tourists and stayed in the Hotel Diplomático in Buenos Aires. We were given a vehicle so that we could travel around. Right after we arrived, a major was assigned to escort us. He coordinated all the activities and brought us to the talks with the General Staff.

Who was more interested in the situation in Central America, General Balín or Captain Davido?

General Balín was very interested in our problems and our points of view. We could speak openly with him. The Captain was very reserved, an analytical type, I'd say. He thought over our arguments very carefully.

With the $50,000 U.S. you received at that time, you could hardly build up an army.

The $50,000 were just to cover absolute necessities. One can hardly build a movement with $50,000. We could pay for our trip with that money.

The cost of supplying Argentine advisers was certainly picked up by the Argentines?

I don't have any information about that.

On the return trip you stopped in Venezuela?

Yes, on the way back we stayed for a couple of days in Venezuela. Chamorro held talks with the Christian-Democratic government of Venezuela. They liked our plans, but, as I said, I wasn't involved in the negotiations because I was only responsible for the military apparatus. Chamorro later characterized the talks as meaningful and successful.

I can't imagine that you didn't discuss the military situation of the organization when you were in Venezuela.

Whether you want to believe it or not, we did not discuss military issues. Some medical supplies were placed at our disposal.

Then you established contact with various Central American embassies. On what level did these talks take place?

In Costa Rica we established contact with officials of the Venezuelan embassy—with the economic attaché and of course also with the military attaché. From Costa Rica they had direct contacts with Nicaragua, but I never asked them how these were maintained. To get back to the original question, from Venezuela we returned to Costa Rica, and Chamorro made his political contacts directly with the Venezuelan embassy or with certain functionaries of the Costa Rican government. In addition, we built our first camp in Honduras, at the Hacienda "El Pescador." It belongs to a Cuban and lies barely 100 kilometers from Tegucigalpa, toward the Nicaraguan border, in the El Paraíso district. Chamorro had good connections with the Honduran military. At that time, the Legion of September 15th organization was already in existence.

How extensive was it?

At first there were only a few people. At that time the UDN-FARN had the best connections with the Honduran capital and with the Honduran military and government. Then, after a while, the UDN-FARN was pushed aside by other groups in Honduras.

Can you tell us more about this development?

It was very important that we did not, under any circumstances, create the impression in Nicaragua that we were working together with the Legion of September 15th. The Legion was entirely composed of ex-National Guards. Naturally one couldn't make a big splash with that in Nicaragua. That's why the Chamorros had no interest in being publicly connected with the Legion. By contrast, the Honduran army had a great interest in supporting its old comrades from the National Guard. And so the Honduran military withdrew its support from Chamorro and gave it to the Legion of September 15th.

The weapons came into your camp with the help of the Honduran Army—weapons that had been purchased in Miami.

That's true, of course. The equipment was brought directly from Miami to Honduras and then distributed to the various camps.

It wasn't necessary to smuggle the weapons out of Miami. They were officially declared to be weapons purchased by the Honduran army, and so they could be brought directly to Tegucigalpa.

The crates were simply shipped from Miami to the Honduran Army?

There was a small firm that bought the weapons and whatever else we needed in the U.S.A. The addressee was the Honduran army. The Honduran consulate in Miami facilitated these transactions.

So it ran like a simple export business?

Naturally that was the easiest way for us. No one had to worry about any shady business; no one had to bribe anyone to keep quiet; everything was legally purchased and shipped.

How many people could you arm at that time?

We were training between 50 and 60 men.

Was there also political instruction at this hacienda, along with the military training?

Actually, there were two camps. Political-military instruction was given in one, using material we had developed ourselves. The most important thing for us was to give the former members of the National Guard and the Somoza sympathizers a new political orientation. Naturally, this was extremely complicated. When someone is over 40 years old, it's hard to change his mentality and his political outlook. The ideological-political education of these people was a waste of time. For most of them, it was clear from the beginning that after a victory things should be exactly as they had been before [under Somoza]. There were also people among them who had fought against Somoza but didn't want to have anything to do with the Sandinistas and so they worked with the UDN.

Did you then return to Nicaragua?

I went back to Nicaragua on December 31, 1981. My specific assignment was to blow up the state cement factory.

How was it possible to bring 300 charges of explosives into Nicaragua?

I never bothered about that. The explosives I needed were already in the country, I don't even know if it was 300 charges.

How was the action planned?

The strategy was economic destabilization of the revolutionary government. It is clear that if one does damage to the economy, this has certain political effects as well. We were therefore trying to stop production at the factory for at least half a year.

How did you proceed? What were you responsible for?

I was just given orders in this action. Even though I had a high military rank, I did not plan it.

So you carried out orders and that was it.

That's exactly it. I got my orders. I was told that I had a certain task to carry out. The plans were already completely worked out. We would then work out the logistics together. As I said, I received the order and had to obey the order. What I needed, of course, was to be able to move around in the country with relative security. This was guaranteed to me. But it didn't correspond to reality.

So you had no safe house, no vehicle, no contacts?

We could not carry out our actions because the "Internal Front" did not exist in reality, only on paper. It was a rather large bluff. On the basis of the reports we received from the Internal Front, we assumed that they had certain cells, safe houses, and that they could move around. But things were really quite different. The crowning blow was that I wasn't even picked up at the appointed place, although it had been previously agreed that a vehicle would wait for me there. That gave me something to think about.

How was the operation to be carried out?

The most important thing was to switch off the cement kilns. We thought that a production shutdown of six months would have to have devastating consequences. We also thought that if at all possible, the workers should not be injured.

How was that possible? It is a really large factory. You couldn't just go in there with explosives under your arm and ask everyone to step outside for a moment.

No, of course not. We assumed that the Internal Front would put certain people from the Granada cell at our disposal. Something like a commando unit. But, to my horror, I discovered that there was absolutely no infrastructure.

What did you do then? Did you try to carry out a part of your plan, or did you look for an alternative?

I went to a contact man at the Venezuelan embassy. I wanted to speak with the military attaché. He told me bluntly that they were not in a position to assume any responsibility for this action. But the attaché did put me in touch with my actual contact person. I met this man two days later. He told me that the entire action was prepared; the people had been trained and sent to certain houses where they were practically waiting for me. We agreed that he would take over the military and I the technical organization. We headed for a place where the contact man wanted to hide the weapons. But we didn't get that far. I lost my contact man again. The time for the sabotage action had almost run out. There were only about ten hours left.

Wouldn't it have been suicide to go ahead with this action?

My problem was that I had a definite order. Therefore I set up another appointment with my contact man to meet Sunday at eight o'clock at a certain place in order to finally decide if, when, and how we could carry out our assignment. When I showed up at eight o'clock at the appointed place, State Security was already waiting for me. The way I was tricked made it clear to me in retrospect that State Security had known about our action beforehand.

Let's assume for a moment that you were able to deposit your explosives at the kilns. I can imagine that there would have been many dead if the cement factory had been blown up.

One can philosophize about that now, but that's not why I was convicted. I haven't heard that this was a reason for convicting those who were going to take part in this act of sabotage.

Would it have been possible to blow up the cement factory without people being injured or killed?

If a commando unit is well-trained and knows its business, then one can make a blitz-action out of it. A commando unit of eight to ten people is, for a certain time, in a position to paralyze all activity. We also assumed that the Frente [FSLN] had not trained the guard personnel there very well. They were members of the militia.

But a couple of hundred workers were employed in the factory.

Yes, but nothing happened, after all. You must know that those who fight the Frente Sandinista in one way or another have to carry out certain actions against the government. These have the purpose of inciting the people to revolt. At the same time, one must take care that such actions are set up by specialists who understand how they should be carried out.

The economic damage that results from sabotage is clear, but the political reaction of the people is not. Wouldn't the hatred of the population more likely be directed against the saboteurs, who destroy what the Sandinista government has built? Or do you believe that the actions of the contras are hailed by the people?

Yes, to a certain extent. But our action was too badly prepared. I've had enough time to analyze the action repeatedly, and I don't believe that it would have achieved the desired results. But what was I supposed to do? I had to carry out an order, otherwise I would have been held responsible. At that time, I could not refuse an order. That is not possible in a clandestine organization.

The groups led by Chamorro have a reputation for not being very disciplined. To disobey an order is, of course, a serious breach of discipline, but was the risk really that great?

I know that the ARDE has shot many soldiers because they wanted to take off. I haven't yet heard of a case in which someone was shot simply because he didn't obey an order. But the organization is not just the person, Chamorro. You can talk with a person. But this was an order to carry out an act of sabotage that was upheld by the whole organization.

I can well imagine that you were politically and personally prepared to take on this action and the consequences.

At the time our organization was supported by various governments, by Honduras and Costa Rica, by the Argentines and Venezuelans. I would not have been able to simply desert and then deposit myself elsewhere. To desert to one of those countries would have meant being arrested immediately.

"The End Justifies the Means"

Conversation with Jorge Ramírez Zelaya

Where were you on July 19, 1979?

I was a member of the 5th Company, called "The Casual," which handled special missions. I had been in this company just a short time, and was only considered to be there temporarily. I had suffered a gunshot wound during the 1978 war and was ill. That is why I was assigned to this unit; I could only go on limited missions. My last service rank was that of lieutenant colonel in the EEBI, the infantry school of Somoza's elite troops.

On July 19, 1979 I had to flee. I fled from the "Campo del Marte" where the 5th Company was located. The top leadership had collapsed, and everyone fended for themselves in our company. I don't know what else was going on in the National Guard.

I fled to the Argentine embassy. That was the only embassy that I was still able to reach. It was located in the section of Managua called "Las Colinas." Life in the embassy went on in a completely normal fashion. We were granted all the rights of political refugees. There were approximately 70 people in the embassy, political refugees and members of their families. Many of them were demoralized, and everyone was trying to leave the country in order to start a new life for themselves. I spent nine months in the embassy, and then I emigrated to Argentina. I went alone, without my family. I stayed in Argentina for 15 months. I worked as a security specialist. Since I had been trained in Argentina, I already had connections there.

What kind of training was that?

I had been sent to Argentina on a government stipend and was trained in providing security for industrial sites.

Why did you leave Argentina the last time?

I was recruited by a member of the FDN staff, by Emilio Echaverry, who is called "El Fierro"—"the man of iron." I had met him in the Argentine embassy. We had been exiles in the same embassy and were compañeros during the war. When I went to Honduras in January 1982, I was his staff assistant.

How was this contact made?

The FDN was in a phase of concentrating all its forces. Before my trip to Argentina, I had been more or less on call. I had been waiting for orders when I went to Argentina, since I had already been in contact with the FDN six months earlier and had received information from them. In early 1982 I travelled to Honduras to join the FDN there.

What sort of training had you had?

I was a graduate of the Military Academy of Nicaragua. In addition, I had taken courses in Panama and Argentina. As a soldier, I was especially interested in secret police activities, heavy weapons, artillery, counterinsurgency, propaganda, guerrilla warfare, sabotage and explosives. After I left the Military Academy, I specialized in security assignments.

Were you also trained as a contra at the 5th School at Ciudad Nueva in Tegucigalpa, which was run by the Argentine military?

I no longer really needed that training. I could brush up on my training there in some ways, although I had already been thoroughly trained. That course of training did make good soldiers for the FDN, and in a short period of time.

Can you remember any of the instructors?

They were really good soldiers, Oswald above all. He was

very tough, very well-disciplined and correct. A military trainer of the best kind.

The FDN recruited some former military men who were staying in Guatemala, El Salvador, Costa Rica, Honduras and the U.S. What was the next step? Didn't you build up and direct the "La Tercera" base?

You are very well informed! My first assignment was as the deputy leader of a base group—a Task Force (Fuerza de Tarea), as these special units were also called. I was in this camp for two months. At that point we had 70 soldiers and were in a setting-up or construction phase.

What was the reaction of the Honduran farmers who lived in the area surrounding the camp?

When I first came to the camp, there was no contact with the population. We were underground. This made it necessary to exercise caution, to take all possible security measures, in order to prevent any infiltration of our troops that could mean information being leaked to the outside. As a matter of principle the camps were not located near villages, but directly on the border. Also, there were no points of friction between the Honduran Army and the FDN. If there had been problems, we certainly wouldn't have been in Honduras. Relations were good, almost fraternal. The members of the 5th Battalion are particularly good people. We visit them often.

Where did the men come from who joined the FDN?

The soldiers were Nicaraguans who were either exiled or had fled to Honduras. Several had been members of the National Guard. Others were simply civilians who had supported the Somoza regime. There were students and also farmers. That was the base. During this period, basic training was standardized and in the course of time it was further perfected. We were still in the building phase. There were still no weapons, no vehicles, no money. We worked with what was there. That was the situation when I arrived in February of 1982.

What was the training like?

In the beginning, everyone got the same training, whether they had come from the National Guard or were students and civilians. Thus the traces that the National Guard had left behind were eradicated. The soldiers were indoctrinated with the mystique of the counterrevolutionary struggle, as it is so beautifully put. It was drummed into them, piece by piece. The primary task was the overthrow of the Sandinista regime. We explained to them that we were dealing with a Communist government, under which human rights were violated, freedom of expression was prohibited, and repressive mass organizations ruled. There was also a wealth of information that the soldiers had to memorize. That was the basic work. You are surely aware of the fact that one finds in these movements people with very varied levels of previous experience and knowledge. We therefore divided them up according to their level of training. The training was carried out by a responsible person from the base. This instructor had himself been trained by the staff of the FDN and took his orders from them. The respective instructors at a base were chosen by the commander.

You said that there were also farmers involved?

We instructed the farmers on the subject of agrarian reform. We told them that the land was being taken away from them and then given to others, in a completely arbitrary way. Yes, this is what we taught them. The farmers were always told that their land would inevitably be expropriated, and that there was only one way for them to oppose this: to take up arms in support of the FDN. But even more important than teaching and indoctrinating the farmers was training them for battle. We could not afford the luxury of first teaching every soldier to read and write. They had a more urgent need for military training and political education.

When did the construction phase of your base actually come to an end?

The first equipment arrived in mid-1982. FAL rifles, 81mm mortars, 50-caliber machine guns, RPG7 grenade launchers, new uniforms, personal equipment items for the individual soldiers —boots, hammocks, backpacks and other necessary items. But there were also radios—at first, Sauco-type radios and PL77 radios. Later we received a large quantity of Yaesu radios, and then Soniers, I think they are Israeli. The first action was carried out in January of 1983 under the code name "Plan C," with massive involvement of all the units that had been trained at the various bases. The assignment was to destabilize the Sandinista regime. Every unit had that hammered into them. The goal was to take Jalapa or any other town in northern Nicaragua.

How is a Task Force, a special unit, structured? Is it similar to those used in Vietnam?

Yes, it is structured like the Task Forces that the Americans used in Vietnam. The Task Forces are divided into groups, and these groups in turn into various commando detachments. Each group has three detachments, and each detachment is made up of 20 soldiers. They are subdivided into various sections, so as to be able to operate in both open country and terrain with cover. This makes the Task Forces enormously well-prepared to react, and mobile in retreating or attacking. Each commando unit has as its basic equipment an M30 machine gun, Law rocket launchers, RPG grenade launchers, a mortar, FAL rifles, AK rifles, and grenades. The weapons have thus been organized in accordance with a new form of distribution. Individual detachments communicate with each other via radio. The detachments are in touch with the groups, and these in turn with the command of the Task Forces. They maintain contact with the radio control stations on the Honduran border. From there, the separate operations can be coordinated, while the Task Forces are simultaneously active in their own zones. Each has a specific mission: to infiltrate, hold a position, attack, pull back, or attack again—in other words, to remain in motion. Thus the creation of the Task Forces is not simply a tactical means of creating larger military units.

Why have they systematically attacked cooperatives, invaded them and taken off with money and food? Was this part of the new strategy in "Plan C?"?

When I was fighting with them, it was a policy of the FDN to attack military targets and individual enemy locations. I don't know whether cooperatives are being attacked now. The Task Forces carry their own food. They also carry enough money to be able to buy what they need in Nicaragua. Each commander takes along several thousand córdobas to take care of his people.

Attacks on cooperatives are routine. Well, O.K. A farmer gives you his only cow and you pay for it. What happens if the Sandinista military then comes along and asks him what happened?

I have no idea! I never took part in Task Force missions. It was my job to organize them, to develop their structure, to supervise the commanders.

I believe that you were also with COTAC, the Command for Tactical Operations on the Atlantic Coast, as an assistant to Major Armando Castellón Falloni and a liaison between the FDN and MISURA. You remained head of the base then.

I would like to tell you something. Steadman Fagoth [head of the counterrevolutionary organization MISURA]* has no conception of what's involved in the art of military work. He is a political leader of the Miskitos. The military leaders were Colonel Justiniano Pe'rez and Major Castellón Falloni, and other officers such as Pavon and "El Merino." My job there was as usual: organization and instruction. The organizational part was exactly

---

* Here, and throughout this book, any text in brackets is explanatory material added for the U.S. edition.

the same, building up Task Forces. The military structure was the same. Only the personnel were different, the officers and soldiers were Miskitos. That was in North Zelaya and along the Atlantic Coast. They only had to be trained, to receive training in secret missions and in taking ground. The base had approximately 800 people. Fagoth put pressure on us to dissolve COTAC. The liaison [between the FDN and MISURA] was eliminated and a greater degree of independence of the administration was established. MISURA now receives everything directly.

Did you have any particular experiences with the Miskitos?

I don't think there is any difference in the learning ability of a Miskito and that of a Latino. Everything was equal, the same information, the same ability to learn, and the same training. With the single difference that there are a great many Miskitos and you have to supervise them more, so that they work somewhat more quickly. But that's of no importance. I was there for 6 months and can report that there were no differences.

As one of the best strategists of the FDN, known as B-1, you were sent by the FDN staff to the Pino-I Base. There the commander called "El Suicida" had brought together about 1800 men who seemed to be beyond his control. The commanders of the other Task Forces wanted an explanation of why "El Suicida," with so many men and weapons, wasn't in a position to take Jalapa. Is it correct that you were supposed to intervene in this situation, and that you also got to know Pedro Javier Núñez Cabezas, "El Muerto," whom you chose as the only one to work with you in preparing and carrying out the M83 plan?

I was there for only 2 weeks, to work out professional plans for "El Suicida" to take Jalapa. But his training wasn't sufficient to carry out this mission, and he also had no discipline. He had attacked much too early, in November, when the mission had not been sufficiently thought out or perfected. He invaded La Providencia on his own and promptly got stuck and then had to take a lot of punishment. I criticized him severely for this. There was no strategic point to this attack, and in addition it was an example of a lack of discipline.

In January, the staff of the FDN wanted me to work out a special plan for him—"Plan Managua '83" or "M83"—in order to strike a serious blow to the Sandinista regime. But that's another story. I was given this assignment and I was trapped. That's how it goes. Plan M83 was sort of an alternative, after the disaster of Plan C. It was part of the overall strategy of the FDN. Simultaneous with the large-scale offensive by the Task Forces in the north, acts of sabotage were to be carried out in Managua. Plan M83 was supposed to destroy important supply lines, to destroy basic logistical facilities of the Sandinista Army and supplies that were supposed to be sent to the northern battle zones. The acts of sabotage in Nicaragua were supposed to damage the refineries, and thus cripple the whole fuel supply and communications. This was intended to touch a particularly sensitive nerve among the combat forces and the air force. I had learned in Panama how to handle the special explosives which are necessary for this kind of action, and then in Honduras, where I refreshed my knowledge. Well, of course I knew how to handle them, but I wanted to familiarize myself once again with all the details.

But you were in Honduras then, you said. How did you get to Nicaraguan territory?

On foot! Yes, on foot. I crossed the border in the west, in the Chinandega zone. In Somotillo a vehicle was waiting for me, which brought me to Managua immediately. All those who supported me logistically were taken into custody. I don't know whether there were others involved.

How many people were involved in the plan? One would surely need several helpers to blow up anything as large as a refinery which, in addition, was located in the middle of the city.

There were two people in charge of the operation. I myself

worked out the strategy and the transfer plan. It was then approved by the staff of the FDN. Of course, we had several members who had been recruited previously in Nicaragua, and who only had to be prepared for the attack. They were supposed to carry out specific data-collecting assignments and make particular preparations. I was only supposed to carry out the thing, to organize it in accordance with the plans we had made.

But this work didn't have much to do with what you have described as your duties with the Task Forces.

This assignment was completely different from what I did with the Task Forces. My job was no longer a directly military job. My job—yes, one can say this—was that of a terrorist. Yes, actually that of a terrorist. It was therefore completely different from what I did in the Task Forces. Being a terrorist means preparing and organizing terrorist actions and sabotage here in Managua. Managua was part of Zone 9, just like the regions in the north which each have a number. Each number is assigned to a commander of a Task Force. I gave the orders in Zone 9, that is, in Managua and the area around it. So you can see from this, too, that the assignment was coordinated with the overall FDN strategy.

As one of those responsible for the "Internal Front," were you also supposed to attack individuals there?

Yes, of course. I was assigned to organize the assassination of various individuals, such as Father D'Escoto, the Nicaraguan Foreign Minister, and Nora Astorga, the Deputy Foreign Minister. Father Ernesto Cardenal was also included. Nora Astorga was among them because she played a large, important part in the murder of a general of the National Guard, the Number 2 man on the general staff, General Sánchez. In addition, she presided over the trials of those who were imprisoned after July 19. We planned to assassinate her to show that she was nothing, that she possessed no moral value, no authority to conduct such a trial.

Cardenal and D'Escoto are members of the Sandinista regime,

and religious men have no business taking government office, in no government of the world. This assassination plan was intended to generate chaos, terror, so that these people who now wear the robes of office would get their hands off. Do you understand this?—and I want to add that everything is interrelated. It is surely no surprise to you that people are killed every day in Asia, Africa, Europe and America. This is always part of the strategy of a particular group, a particular movement.

But the FDN wants to take political power. Aren't you afraid of being rejected by the populace because of the terrorism?

It is surely clear to you, too, that terrorism exists throughout the world. It isn't as if we started it here in Nicaragua. It must, of course, be clear that terrorism is always political, always a political instrument.

But doesn't the FDN believe that its national and international image will be weakened or damaged by these terrorist actions?

No, I don't think so. There is a psychological blow, with a great propaganda effect nationally and internationally, that justifies these actions. The end justifies the means—that's all I can say.

The FDN is kept functional by the financial and military support of the U.S. government. Does it also support terrorist actions?

It is absolutely clear that the movement, any underground movement, is able to survive only with the support of a continental power. Let me give the following example: Arafat is supported by Libya, there is no doubt about this, and we are supported in the same way by the United States. Every revolution is supported by a foreign power.

How are you supported?

With comprehensive financial aid, with weapons, and with war materiel, in sufficient quantity since 1982. This support is channeled through the CIA, through a North American named Mike, Mike Tock. He is responsible, as an officer, for operations within the FDN. He gets the money and the weapons. He also has an assistant, he's called Alex, but I can't remember exactly— Alex the American. In addition, we also receive support from a group in Argentina. They are responsible for advising the various groups, for training them or giving them special orders. . . .

And why is this? How are the leaders of the FDN trained?

All of the commanders of the Task Forces have had a complete military education, as have the general staff. But there are also intermediate service ranks, group leaders, who have been trained just as well and who have been tested in battle. They receive regular, additional training, in order to operate within Nicaraguan territory.

Why is it that in Latin America these military personnel are called gorillas?

O.K., now I have to make something perfectly clear! I would like to make it clear that there are no gorillas in any army in Latin America. I don't know where this expression comes from, hairy soldiers with clubs. I was trained as a soldier in Panama and received specialized training after my three years of training at the Military Academy in Nicaragua. In Panama I expanded upon everything I had learned, technically and theoretically. I did all of this in order to enter the service of my country after having received this comprehensive training, just like military men do in the U.S. and in Argentina. Everyone who was in the National Guard had the same, perfect training. This has nothing whatsoever to do with being a gorilla.

If that's true, then why did you lose the war when you had such excellent troops?

But that is perfectly obvious. Because of the blockade— economic, political and military—which was imposed on us during the 1970's, the total blockade by the U.S. All of the equipment we had came from the U.S. Then this Jimmy Carter suddenly started up with all his nonsense about human rights. He cut off all of our support. Luckily, Carter's policies are now being corrected by President Reagan.

Do you mean that President Reagan should put everything in order...?

No, no. I am interested in Nicaragua, not in Jimmy Carter or President Reagan. But we're not having any problems with support now. That's how things are at the moment. As I've already said, every underground movement is supported and financed by some other country. I only hope that this conflict ends soon.

The FDN once stated that it would cost 15,000 dead to win. Or do you think the Sandinistas would simply give up their power?

I never said anything about their simply giving up power. All I want is for those who are now living in exile to be allowed to return unhindered to Nicaragua. I don't expect to be accepted back into the military. No, I don't expect that, even though I am a professional soldier, a specialist. But I'm not interested in that. I'm interested in Nicaragua. Everyone must have the right to return to Nicaragua. Everyone who is in exile wants to live here again. As Nicaraguans we have a right to this. We are Nicaraguans, it's only logical.

But what would happen to all those who are responsible for criminal offenses?

These things are normal in all liberation movements, this is the case everywhere. But it is also clear that propaganda is an extraordinarily important medium and is controlled by those who have the money and who know how to play this instrument. I believe that all Nicaraguans in exile long for national reconciliation. They want to see their country again and be reunited with their families. In this connection, the FDN has taken a political position; it wants to take part in the elections. These are the proposals which have been made by the political leadership, to strive for national reconciliation. This is also being supported by the opposition parties. They, and all those in exile, want to take part in the elections in order to elect the new President of Nicaragua. I don't see this as anything unusual.

Do you believe that the FDN will win the war?

It is clear to me that the FDN cannot win the war; that is logical. The FDN is there to destroy the Sandinistas. The FDN is a political-military destabilization movement, which has developed a strategy aimed at national reconciliation. It wants nothing more than to exercise its power so that the political leaders who are now in exile can take part in the elections and can all return. It isn't necessary to change what now exists there, what has already been done. If it's good, there is no reason for that.

I don't understand that.

Then I will explain it in more detail. I have already said that we want to return to Nicaragua, to a Nicaragua without Somoza, that is clear. [Nicaragua with Somoza] no longer exists. If there is an election now, some candidate will win. There are reforms. Any change in government is accompanied by reforms, which only makes sense. One of these new reforms will be that everyone who is exiled can return to Nicaragua, that we can move about freely in Nicaragua, so that there is peace and democracy.

Yes, that makes it somewhat clearer. If candidate X wins, there will be reforms which will make it seem that there is no longer a need for the CDS, along with obligatory military service, the mass organizations, agrarian reform, educational reform, university reform. Is that how it would be?

I don't know what reforms there would be, but those are certainly the most important ones. I can't say anything about these reforms, I'm not a politician.

If you say that the end justifies the means, then what is the actual goal?

The actual goal is returning to Nicaragua.

"Orders Are There To Be Carried Out"

Conversation with Pedro Javier Núñez Cabezas

What were you doing in July 1979?

At the time of the revolt, I was living in Managua. I was in high school at the time. I didn't take part in the revolt, I was still in school, and for me that meant just learning.

How old were you, and what high school did you attend?

I was 18 at the time and in the fifth class at the "February 1st" Institute.

Isn't that the institute attended by sons of higher state officials and members of the National Guard?

Yes, that's correct.

What happened then on July 19?

On July 18, I went together with my family to the Guatemalan embassy and asked for asylum. My mother decided that. My father was no longer alive; he'd been a first lieutenant in the National Guard. My mother and my two sisters thought it would be best to ask for asylum in the Guatemalan embassy. My mother's father and all her brothers had worked for the Somoza government. My two brothers were majors in the Somozan air force. We stayed in the embassy six months with many other asylum-seekers. We had nothing to do and played chess all day. On December 31, 1979, we were granted safe-conduct and went at once to Guatemala.

I wanted to study agricultural engineering, but it wasn't possible there. In Guatemala we didn't have enough money to pay for my studies. It was also hard to find work. It was even harder for foreigners, especially for a Nicaraguan. One can live on the minimum wage in Guatemala, more or less. But there's no way to pay for an education on it.

In this situation, I established contact with other Nicaraguans. There were many of them, and for the first time I heard that some wanted to return to Nicaragua. Well, that's how it all started. I hooked up with my first contacts through an acquaintance. I joined FRENICA, the Nicaraguan Revolutionary Front. FRENICA was a political-military organization that was setting up an underground organization.

Who was in charge of FRENICA?

In Guatemala, Colonel Lau—we called him "the Chinese"— was behind everything. I fully joined FRENICA, left home, abandoned my work, and quickly lost all contact with my family. I began to prepare my return to Nicaragua.

How were you trained?

It was completely military, and directly from FRENICA. I received theoretical and practical training. I was instructed at a safe house in the B-zone of Guatemala and at the Aurora Airport. After that we were transported to a small village, Esquipulas, right on the border of Honduras. There were 40 of us altogether who prepared exclusively for the military.

Had you been interested in that before July 19?

No, not at all. In Guatemala, I thought for the first time of getting organized when I saw the situation my family and I were in. We were in a country where we received no form of support, neither moral nor financial. I couldn't just return to Nicaragua because I had left the country under a safe conduct, as an asylum-seeker at the embassy.

But you had gone to the embassy of your own free will; you weren't guilty of anything?

Yes, that's true, but as I already said, I was completely dependent upon my mother. She had decided for me.

But if that's true, couldn't you have stayed without any difficulty?

Yes, of course, but my mother wore the pants. There was no arguing, I had to obey her.

Before that I didn't know anything about military training. We received instruction in physical fitness, battle positions, how to lay an ambush, how to plan an attack—everything one needs for basic military training, so that one survives in battle.

In which countries were you trained?

Besides Guatemala and Honduras, also in Argentina. In our commando unit, and I'm talking now about those 40 men, I was the one with the best education. That was the real thing that differentiated me from the others. They chose me for further instruction in Argentina. Colonel Lau took care of the passports and visas, everything we needed. I was the only one from our group. The others who travelled with me were all ex-officers of the National Guard. There were almost no civilians. There were also a couple of students who lived in the U.S. and who still had family members in Nicaragua who were affected by the situation. Some were sons of former military men who were sitting in jail. And there were others who didn't want to accept the situation in Nicaragua. Some had family members in prison. Some had political worries but, as I said, most of us were officers in the National Guard.

In Argentina we were trained at a safe house. It was in Buenos Aires, in a residential district about half an hour from Ezeiza Airport. The training was purely theoretical; there was no practical instruction. We were taught theories of espionage, counterespionage, interrogation techniques, beating techniques [the speaker did not use the word torture], how to lead troops, and psychological warfare.

Secret service work was to become my specialty. In this area, the training was intended to teach how best to gather information, how to make decisions in certain situations, what kinds of security measures an organization has to take so that it won't leave any information behind for the enemy.

We were brought together in the province of Buenos Aires. Civilians picked us up at the airport, put us in a car, and brought us to the safe house.

Were the civilians members of the Argentine secret service?

I think they were from the Argentine secret service. Our training goal was set. We were to carry out secret service assignments in Nicaragua. Everyone who went to Argentina at that time was part of, or rather, a member of a new organization called the Legion of September 15th.

I really enjoyed learning the material. I thought everything they taught was very interesting. Instruction was given by members of the Argentine military. Personal contact with them, however, was impossible; they always came to class punctually, explained everything clearly and well, and then they were gone again. Colonel Corea, Captain Pérez, and Lieutenant Mora, who taught us about secret service work, were excellent. But none of us could build a close relationship with them. The course was very intensive, with a full schedule: nine hours a day, plus homework. It lasted one month, from February to March. I didn't see anything of Buenos Aires. We weren't allowed out of the safe house.

When the course was over, we were brought directly back to the airport and sent immediately to Guatemala. At the airport, I was picked up by Benito Bravo, my superior, and was brought to a safe house in the "Cerro de Hule" district of the city. The new organization, the Legion of September 15th, divided us up into working groups and handed out various assignments. A couple of the groups travelled to Miami; others—no, I don't know where they went. I was assigned to the group that was to build camps in Honduras.

You said that in the course of this the movement changed names.

FRENICA was held together by ex-National Guard members and civilians, the only organization that really had a structure and also trained its members. Sometimes Francisco Urcuyo, the President installed by Somoza, came by. But FRENICA had difficulties with the Guatemalan military, which was giving us financial support. The National Guard members had problems, too. So people changed it from FRENICA to the Legion of September 15th. The Legion was under the command of Colonel Enrique Bermúdez. With this influx, the organization took on a new, solid appearance. Up to that point, American support was still very modest. At the beginning, the Legion went through a phase in which it hardly received any support. The gringos made no secret of the fact that if we wanted support from them, we'd first have to join forces with the FDN [Fuerza Democrática Nicaragüense, Nicaraguan Democratic Force].

How is it that you know so much about these details?

I already knew all of this before I went to Argentina. Yes, I already knew then what the situation was: the difficulties the other groups had to face—no food, no clothing. Everything we needed was in short supply, especially weapons. Our leaders told us why everything was so scarce. They explained to us what was going on. Colonel Enrique Bermúdez, who commanded the Legion, told us everything.

Did you receive any other instruction besides the courses you've already told us about?

You mean ideological? No, there was no political instruction, just pure military training. I didn't think that the other stuff was necessary.

Didn't you have political discussions among yourselves? About the developments in Nicaragua, for example, the agrarian reform or the other changes the Sandinistas carried out?

My decision to work with the contras was largely determined by my family's financial situation and, from reports, I knew that Communism was reigning in Nicaragua. For me, Communism is the same thing as totalitarianism. It takes everything people need to live and does away with it. Communism seizes everything for itself, with the goal of enslaving the people.

Those were actually the two main reasons I decided to join the contras.

You said before that they selected you to set up camps. How, and with what resources?

As I already said, from Guatemala I went to Honduras to set up and organize camps—on the Honduran side, naturally, very close to the border of Nicaragua. In Guatemala and Honduras we used public transportation like normal citizens—unarmed, of course. In Guatemala I took a bus to the border of Honduras, crossed the border, and took another bus to Tegucigalpa. In Tegucigalpa I had an address, so I took a taxi to the house, gave the pass- and code-words, and was let in. The whole group, which was comprised of people coming from different parts of Honduras, met in this house to organize the camps.

Setting up a camp is nothing more than organizing a certain number of people to come together at a certain place and training them with the goal of being able to penetrate Nicaraguan territory. That means massive organizing, efforts to persuade, and building support networks. After that one can start establishing safe houses. Only toward the end does one actually start setting up a camp. For most of the assignment, you yourself are responsible; you have to determine the site. Then, when the first people come, you have to start setting up right away. All this still happens without weapons. We don't need them yet, either. We are, after all, on Honduran territory, and no one's going to attack us.

The support of the gringos really started coming in after the building of the FDN was completed. After March, 1982 the FDN received every conceivable kind of support from the gringos: weapons, money, everything one needs. In March, the green stuff came: the weapons, the uniforms, the boots, the backpacks, the cartridge belts. All of it new, good material. Everything came directly from the gringos. Yes, that's how it was. But before that, when there were financial problems, nothing happened, no action. So I went to Costa Rica, where I had family. Then I received new information.

Wasn't that at the time when Radio Continental was damaged by an attempted bombing in which the FDN took part?

At that time I was at Camp "La Cruz" with Alberto Toruño. I had met him in Argentina. The Civil Guard of Costa Rica seized us and deported us to Panama. The organization then sent me from Panama to Venezuela. In Venezuela we received passports, money and everything else we needed and were sent back to Honduras to meet Abel, the leader of the Military Secret Service of the FDN. In August, 1982, the staff of the FDN sent me from there to the Pino-I Base, where I was in charge of the Military Secret Service, at the side of Comandante "El Suicida." I became Chief of the Secret Service because I had been trained for it and because I had the ability to analyze situations. I still wasn't made a comandante because I had no battle experience. The rank of comandante, that is, commander, was taken by ex-members of the National Guard. But because I had been in the contras a relatively long time, they told me I would be promoted pretty damned fast, since I was so intelligent. Also, they couldn't treat me like a dog anymore, like someone who was just starting. I believe they thought me capable of being responsible for the Secret Service.

My assignment was to get information about the situation of the Sandinista army and about the region I was in charge of—Nueva Segovia. Then I had to evaluate it. There were no problems in gathering the information. Then I worked on it, analyzed it, and informed Comandante "El Suicida." He had to decide, on the basis of discussing the situation, what was to be done. I instructed him about the situation of the enemy in the area of operations so that he could decide how to proceed. Everything was his decision.

Who gathered this information?

On the base I had specially trained personnel from the Nueva Segovia region who knew the area and also had contacts inside the country to give them information. I gave my people certain assignments; they gathered the information and turned it over to me.

With all this I built a real archive, we could call it, about the various positions of the enemy, or better, a map of where the enemy was located and its positions. I had my office at the Pino-I Base and also my own people who went over the border into Nicaragua, made contacts, and brought back information which I then evaluated and passed on with recommendations.

Did you also take part in a larger military action?

In November-December, 1982, I took part in a march from Honduras into Nicaraguan territory, into La Providencia Valley. Comandante "El Suicida" led the operation. We remained in Nicaragua more than 25 days. Then we had to return because we were holding a position that didn't gain us anything. No reason, therefore, to let ourselves be wiped out.

The march into Nicaraguan territory, and the stay there, took place entirely under the orders of "El Suicida." He was the commander. He determined what had to be done and what had to be abandoned, even if he was wrong. We went over with 200, almost 300 people, who then divided themselves up into fighting units of twenty each. I had to find out where the Sandinista forces were camped and how they were operating, and I had to think about whether they could attack us.

I believe that we weren't pursuing a realistic goal with this invasion. After the first skirmishes, the residents left the area immediately and the only people who stayed were the FDN and the Sandinista troops. So we also couldn't carry out any armed propaganda [acts carried out by an armed force to create identification of the populace with members of that force and the weapons they carry]. La Providencia is a residential area. The peasants who lived there and were organized had moved to Jalapa. Therefore most of us decided right away to go to Jalapa. The others went back to Honduras.

From what we have heard, these encroachments were supposed to aid in recruiting new fighters. It has been said that this often happened violently.

Of those we had to remove by force when I was along, some belonged to the CDS or were informers, or both. We took them along and slapped them around a bit, and did away with them. To bring them along [as recruits] by force is pointless; they're unreliable. Imagine if you had to go along with 60, 70 or 80 recruits who followed you only if they were forced to, with 5 or 6 among them who really wanted to fight. They'd take off right away with the weapons, or take a stand against you, or something like that. So you don't bring anyone along by force. That's how it was when I was there. We are talking about 1982.

Were you paid?

Only the most important people were given financial support, such as the comandantes of the Task Forces and also the urban members of the FDN. Their ranks go from S1 to S5. This support was intended for the families, for the children.

Did you get money as well?

They gave me money for the logistical things I needed, for the Secret Service, and 200 lempiras [Honduran currency] for my personal needs.

*You said before that peasants who belonged to the defense com-
mittees of the revolution, the CDS, or who supported the Sandinista army, were simply eliminated—that couldn't have been
universal? Wasn't that murder? There must have been mistakes,
too.*

Everyone at the Pino-I Base, where I was stationed, were from
the zone we operated in, and they knew who was who. They told
us who was a member of the CDS, or who was an informer, or
whatever else they did.

But why members of the CDS?

That happened by order of the commander; he makes all the
decisions. He gives the directives. Every man is responsible for
his zone. The commander gives orders to the group leaders of
the raiding parties and tells them what to do in these cases.

*Have you yourself ever killed anyone just because he was a CDS
member?*

Of course, but only under military orders. You see, I know
what you're trying to get at. One day on the mountain at Guam-
buco, four militia members and a couple by the name of Barreda
were captured. There was a skirmish between the Sandinista army
and a raiding party from the Pino-I Base. Then they brought these
people to Honduran territory. The comandante in charge informed
us about his catch, and "El Suicida" ordered him to bring them
all to the base.

What for?

As I already told you, those are decisions of the comandante.
It was reported to me that the *milicianos* gave themselves up, and
that the couple gave themselves up after we caught them in an
ambush. The man had been hit by some shrapnel. They were seized
and brought to Honduran territory, where they were interrogated.

What techniques are used to carry out such an interrogation?

That's not my field. The tactics used in conducting an interrogation depend entirely on the person doing it. Very often, indirect interrogation is used. That means the person who is to be interrogated doesn't even know that it's happening. Direct interrogation is introduced once the subject knows that he is being interrogated.

What would you do if, for example, I did not want to talk?

You would be beaten until you talked. Also, an interrogation is carried out intensively only when it can be determined that the subject can give information of interest. No time is wasted interrogating people who can't give any information. CDS members, for example, don't usually give any useful information. So they aren't interrogated. They're eliminated right away. A real interrogation is useful only if one has captured a soldier in battle. Then one can get information from him that's directly applicable.

And if I don't want to talk?

Then you have to suffer the consequences. You know that you're my enemy. You were seized with a weapon, in a battle zone, and so you know that you have to cooperate in order to avoid more trouble.

And if I don't say a word in spite of all that, and even get angry, what do you as an officer of the FDN do?

Then you're liquidated. A lot of different factors come into play that can't be overlooked. In war, one can't waste a lot of time with long interrogations. A person either says what he knows, or bears the consequences and is eliminated.

To return to the prisoners, what happened to those at the Pino-I Base in Honduras?

It's different in Honduras; it depends on the person in charge of the interrogation. Let's assume that time is on my side. Then the interrogated person is always the loser. He has to stew in his own juices for that time. It depends only on the interrogated, only on him. If you are left for a couple of days without food, for example, then I am working with something that no human being can endure. That is, there are times when one doesn't have to beat up anybody, or touch anybody, or torture anybody. And in spite of that, you'll talk.

Is it always that way?

One can find out pretty quickly by the behavior of the inter-rogated. One can see right away how the other person behaves. One also knows if he will talk or if he will keep his lips sealed, whether he dies or not. But I don't have much experience with this kind of interrogation. The only thing I can say is that no time is wasted on the CDS...

How was the interrogation with the Barreda couple done?

The comandante, who operated in the Seibón zone, a coffee zone, as you know, wired that he had captured four militiamen and two big fish. It would be a little while before they returned. I was present at this interrogation. But it was conducted by L67, "El Tigre," a man by the name of Tijerino. He was from the headquarters of the FDN Secret Service and was previously an interrogator in the Somozan Secret Service. He beat them up right away. Then someone else came; he was the adjutant of "El Suic-ida." He had also been in Argentina and had attended all the classes and therefore knew that it is not easy to make people talk by means of physical torture. He used a different method. He said that they should be left to sleep naked all night long, outside in the pouring rain. That's the kind of thing that will break anyone's resolve and make him forget resistance. Just like hunger, or a host of other techniques, most of them psychological. That is what I under-stood at the time and that is the kind of technique that was employed. The pair was hardly captured when "El Suicida" informed the staff. The staff has special people for this and sent them right away. Then some people from the September 15th Radio Station also came, who had video cameras with them. What this couple, who were in the hands of the FDN, would say was considered important.

Some of the militia members were able to flee and later said that Mrs. Barreda was the victim of a gang rape. She hemorrhaged shortly after that. Her husband could no longer walk and was dragged around the camp behind a horse.

When I was there, that didn't happen. You can believe me. I heard that she was hemorrhaging and that she was sick, but more than that I don't know. Certainly they were both exhausted when they arrived at the camp [Mrs. Barreda was about 60 years old and had arthritis]. The place where they had been captured was a long way from there. They were caught in an ambush, but I already mentioned that. Whether or not she was raped at the camp, I can't say.

The CDS and others were liquidated on the spot by the leaders of the troops. I liquidated the couple, but only on "El Suicida's" orders. In this case "El Suicida" had the last word.

But you certainly can't tell us that your word didn't carry any weight. Weren't you a member of the officer corps?

Yes, that's true; I had rank, but there were problems between the comandantes and the rest of the corps. It's a question of command authority. Perhaps it's because they can tell that someone is more capable than someone else, or something like that, but there is always friction. "El Suicida" was one of those types who wanted absolute command authority. I couldn't even send my own people out to gather information, on my orders, even though I knew how important it was. He alone gave the orders. I couldn't just say, go and get me information from this or that area. I had to ask "El Suicida" first, and ask him as the superior officer to give the command. So it was he who gave it. He didn't get involved any further; he gave the order to liquidate, looked on and said nothing. Then I shot the Barredas through their heads with a 9mm Browning.

The Barredas were Sandinistas and practicing Catholics. Is it true that they wanted to pray first?

Everyone has his own belief. Each person does what his belief tells him to; each acts according to his conscience. I'm a Christian. I'm a Catholic.

I don't understand that. For you, catechism is one thing and the job is another?

That's right. As I understand it, when someone is in the middle of a situation, he alone has to evaluate the danger he's in and consider the consequences. And he makes the decision because he knows the consequences and then has to make the best of it. When I get an order, such as we have just discussed, I can't refuse it. I'd be arrested, then they'd put handcuffs on me.

That's supposed to be the explanation?

I believe in fate. I was supposed to be captured; therefore I was captured.

What do you do now?

I'm teaching chess to my colleagues in jail, and they're slowly beginning to master it. That's how we kill time. My brother brings me books, a brother who lives here in Managua. Right now I'm reading a book about the evolution of life by someone named Oparion, a Russian. He talks mostly about dialectical materialism. I'm reading him to kill time. I've already read a couple of books here about the future of society, or novels by Sir Arthur Doyle, Agatha Christie, that kind of thing.

"There Are Many Women Who Work in the Camp and Are Given Military Training"

Conversation with a Honduran woman

I come from the port of La Ceiba. I'm a Honduran woman. My mother always wanted me to go to school and make something of myself, but after third grade I'd had enough. I didn't get along with my mother at all anymore, so I just ran away from home. I wanted to stand on my own two feet and work for myself, not for other people. When I was only 17, I already had my own business—a small bar. But what sticks to us women like a curse is that we're all weak and let ourselves be swept away by love. Men know our weakness and take advantage of it. My story is the story of this feminine weakness. I let myself be swept off my feet by a man, and I followed him wherever he wanted to go.

That sounds like the beginning of a dime-store novel. Perhaps you could be a little bit more concrete.

This man I'm talking about was a Nicaraguan, a real sweetheart. One day he sat at my counter and watched me the whole time. That was nothing new. The men in the bar undressed women with one glance. They'd drink a couple of shots and leave. The Nicaraguan came regularly, either alone or with friends. He was a good-looking man; I liked him.

Did he tell you what he did? How he earned his money?

He was a soldier and had served in the Nicaraguan National Guard before. He said he loved me. He was good to me; I thought he was serious. He told me a lot about his country—that there was a government in power there which was very aggressive and would maybe even attack my country one day. But I was not interested in those political things at all. For me it was important that he liked me and that he was serious and that he didn't just want to take advantage of me.

He was honest with me and said that for him the time had come when he couldn't hang around in Tegucigalpa any longer. Instead he had to fight again for Nicaragua, for his ideals.

What did that mean for your relationship?

I didn't want to let him go. I wanted to go with him, I wanted to be with him, and so he took me along to the military camp a couple of kilometers away from Trojes. It was called Arenales. That was in January, 1983. A woman in the camp was not really unusual. There were a lot of Nicaraguan women who worked in the camp or were given military training. In my group there were only three women; I am not counting the ones who worked in the kitchen, they were older. I don't know much about the other women. They were in other training groups. I can only remember one; her name was Valdivia, or something like that. Her brother was also in the FDN. Another brother died from a bullet wound.

How was camp life? Could you continue to live with your boyfriend?

There were about 700 people in the camp. I could stay with my boyfriend, that was no problem. For a couple of days I just looked around to see what the situation was. I decided to take part in the instruction, the training, in everything the men did. Without my being really aware of how my life was changing, I wore a uniform and carried an AK. I was also trained in the use of this Russian weapon.

The change must have been pretty drastic—one day in a bar and then the next day in military training.

At first the pants we had to wear every day bothered me. I hadn't worn pants very often before, but here everyone wore the same thing. I couldn't step out of line. The training was the same for men and women. Age made no difference; 12- and 14-year-old youths were trained alongside 40- and 50-year-old men. We had to do physical training so that we'd be able to make it through the long foot marches with backpacks and all the supplies. In spite of everything, my training was very short; it only lasted a month.

You received no political instruction?

I was supposed to go with one of the fighting units and when it was just about ready to set out, a group of people from the political administration arm of the FDN came and informed us about what was going on in Nicaragua at the time. They explained to us why we were fighting and said that the goal was to overthrow the Communist government in Nicaragua. They told us that the state was taking everything away from the peasants who had worked their whole lives and owned a little livestock, and that it was taking over private property, houses for example, and that there was no religious freedom.

Were there regular church services in the camp, and priests for spiritual advisers?

When I was in camp, three priests visited us. I'm a devout Catholic, but there are also many who say they're Catholic even though there's nothing behind it; they only move their lips when they pray. I went to a Catholic school, although I was really one of those who would rather stand in front of the church than go inside. My heart was never really in it. That was when I was young, however; now I need the Catholic faith. The priests gave their little enlightening talks when the people from the political arm of the FDN were there. Beyond that there were three masses celebrated during the month; the last one was before we went over the border. At that one we also received a blessing. The priests told us horror stories about Nicaragua; that many people had left the country because there was no religious freedom, that many had their land taken away and all their property, that still others had left the country because they had relatives who used to be in the National Guard or were in jail, and because of that they were made to suffer or their children were put in the militia.

How did you get across the border into Nicaragua?

Our first big obstacle was crossing the Río Coco. We divided up into various groups beforehand. There were 400 of us. One group with M15 and M60 machine-guns went ahead to secure the crossing. The river wasn't very deep. We could cross it on foot. I was horrified to see what was waiting for me: gun over my head, backpack under water, and all those supplies suddenly tripling in weight. A month of training is simply not enough to be able to endure the physical hardship. A lot of things went through my head: if I wouldn't be better off just turning around and forgetting about all this stuff. I regretted having gone along, but it was also clear to me that I couldn't just take off. They called that desertion, and the penalty was death. They would rather kill us than let us fall into the hands of the Sandinistas, who would brutally torture and then kill us. After more day-long marches than I could count, I was completely wiped out—we were very close to Wamblan, already a good distance inland, and I simply could not go any further. I threw away everything I could and just held onto the gun and a couple of rounds of ammunition.

We were already at least one and a half kilometers away from the fighting unit; with me were two young guys, peasants, who also didn't feel like marching anymore. They had been carried off by an FDN troop a while back, brought to the camp, and trained to fight against the government. I wondered about the fact that they were so trusting of me, but I think we just didn't have to pretend to each other anymore; we were at the end of our rope. After we had rested a couple of hours and gathered some of our strength, my husband came looking for me. I made it clear to him that there was no way I could go any further, and that I also lacked the strength to stick it out in a battle. We thought about what we could do. The peasants came from the neighboring area and promised to help us. What we needed was civilian clothing. They said it would be no problem. We left the weapons behind and took off to look for civilian clothes. That's when they caught us. My husband could still talk himself out of the situation, but the fact that I was a foreigner, a Honduran, was easy to see from how I talked.

When you think back about it today, what's your opinion of it all?

I made a mistake; that's clear to me. But I'm not going to drive myself crazy because of it. My family doesn't know what's going on at all. I believe they actually think I'm dead. At any rate, they have no idea what kind of a mess I'm in. I didn't want to talk to the ambassador, either; who knows what they would have used my situation for. Of course, in prison there are certain things you have to put up with. The war, the destruction, all that has its effects. The food is skimpy—beans and rice, and that's it. What impresses me is that the guards eat the same thing we do. What I don't understand—and I've already asked several times that we political prisoners be allowed to work. The political prisoners are those who, whether or not they want to, get hung up in situations they can't handle later on. It's interesting to see what falls under "political prisoner." I only really know that I was given arms, assigned to a fighting unit, and that I came to Nicaragua. But I don't understand anything about politics. Everyone's afraid of the political prisoners. There are many women here who tell me what they did and why they were punished, and that they would do the same thing over again tomorrow. The other prisoners all keep their distance from us because they think we would give them an earful. What I want to do is work. I have to do something with my hands to make the time pass. To hang around all day and sit on a mattress, that really finishes you off.

"With God and Patriotism, We Will Overthrow Communism"

Reports from
Eduardo López Valenzuela and
Miguel Angel Jiménez Bautista

I am Eduardo López Valenzuela, a member of an FDN unit commanded by Rubén. In former times, I always worked in the fields, cultivating corn and beans. I did not join anybody. I went from home to work, from work to home. At most I sometimes went shopping to buy just the necessities like coffee, soap. I was recruited in Wiwilí by Ramón Zeledón, whose code name is "Maravilla," which means miracle. There were eight of us in one group, commanded by Taolamba. The eight men were Lázaro, El Zañate, Maravilla, Catalino, El Zorro—I don't remember the names of the other two men.

We marched toward El Plátano. Beltrán Vásquez and Santos Gonzáles, two farmers from this area, helped us. Eight days passed and then we were ordered to go to Zompopera. We were to stay there to help prepare Richard's passage into Honduras.

After one week we met Rubén at a previously agreed-on place, still inside Zompopera territory. We killed a pig and ate it together. "Cinco Pinos" disappeared with his men in the direction of Honduras. We marched with Rubén, 200 men, and arrived at Don Pancho's. There we ate a calf. Then we started to prepare ourselves for our work in Zompopera. We killed two cows and ate them. In the afternoon, Raúl Rodríguez arrived with a mulatto who was carrying 200 córdobas worth of baked goods. We ate them, then Raúl took Rubén aside. I suppose they were talking about what we were going to do in the coming days.

At 3 a.m. Rubén called us together to listen to a speech. He ordered us to build a barricade on the road between Zompopera and Pantasma. We arrived there at 4:30 a.m. and started to work on the roadblock. Soon we had finished it, and then we started the ambush. Some cars were caught. First a light blue IFA arrived and was stopped by the roadblock. Some of us climbed up to push the IFA down the hill. Five minutes later, a small truck arrived but we were not prepared to stop it. Then a truck came that was loaded with bottles of lemonade. We grabbed the lemonade and drank it.

At that moment a blue jeep appeared with 13 people in it. All 13 got out and stood in a line before us. There were three nurses among them. Jimmy Leo, Polo, and Rubén immediately began to rape the three women. The women implored them to stop but nobody cared. After the rape, they fired a volley of 20 shots with an FAL into the head and chest of each woman.

Then Jimmy Leo marched up to a man who looked like a foreigner. The man said, "Stop shooting! We are civilians. I am a physician from Germany. Don't kill us!" Jimmy didn't let this bother him. And as the foreigner cried out again, "Don't kill us!" Jimmy Leo began firing at him, from the head down to the chest.

After he finished firing into the doctor's head and chest, Jimmy Leo turned to me, Eduardo López Valenzuela. "Now it's your turn," he commanded. So then I also went and killed a person who was wearing blue trousers and a white shirt. With an AKA, I fired one shot after another—five shots into the head and another five into the chest.

We were satisfied when they were all dead. We were happy and shouted again and again, "With God and patriotism we will overthrow Communism," and "Viva the FDN!" Ramón Zeledón shouted, and Rubén shouted, and Taolamba shouted: "Nicaragua is full of Communists, we must defeat the Communists. Nothing but Communists in Nicaragua! We must expel them." Again and again we shouted together, "Viva the FDN!"

Our celebration was interrupted by the arrival of a red jeep with a white roof. Two persons were sitting inside, one a dark type, the other more white. We fired immediately. They tried to crawl out of the car, starting to fire back. They hit Taolamba, and Jimmy Leo got shot in the rear. We fired as much as we could, with M-79s, 60-mm mortars, hand grenades. We shot the lighter man in the arm. He ran in the direction of Pantasma. A hundred meters further he fell down, but then ran on. Six of us followed him, the pregnant La Pelona, El Gato, El Zorro, Maravilla, Lázaro, El Zañate. La Pelona and El Gato got him. El Gato put out the man's eyes with an iron stick, then ransacked his pockets to see what he had. There was a briefcase and 300 córdobas. El Gato also ripped off the man's boots. Rubén said to La Pelona and Gato, "That was a big fish we got."

Meanwhile, a Nicaraguan army truck had arrived and Lázaro ordered us to retreat. Only a few meters farther, Taolamba died. Hidden by bushes, we marched in the direction of Zompopera. At 3 p.m. we buried Taolamba. We crossed the Río Coco, killed two cattle and ate them.

Postscript

Report by
Miguel Angel Jiménez Bautista

I know Jimmy Leo well—yes, that's what he calls himself. I invaded Nicaragua with the "Jorge Salazar" fighting unit, which is under the command of "Renato." We came from Honduras and marched into the area around Wamblancito. In La Minita we set up camp and prepared ambushes. Franklin's troop joined us. After three days' marching we came to the highway that leads to Waslala. We were supposed to back up Toño's fighting unit. That was our assignment. During the night we made it to the

Hacienda La Florida. There's also a small camp there. Then every troop set out for where it had been ordered to go.

I had sprained my foot. It was very swollen, and I stayed in La Florida. We cleared mines off a hectare of land because a helicopter carrying weapons, ammunition, uniforms, and boots was expected. It needed a small landing pad. In the camp, about 60 men were being trained. One of the instructors was Jimmy Leo; they called the other one "Primitivo." We were not through cleaning off the terrain when we were fired upon and had to take off as fast as we could. Jimmy Leo took off, too.

"I'm a Real Expert..."
Conversation with
Roberto Amador Narváez

What were you before the Sandinistas took power?

I was in the Air Force. I joined in about 1960, I don't know exactly anymore, but it was during the time of Luis Somoza Debayle. After I had performed my duties for some time as an officer candidate, I was sent to the United States for training as a pilot. I passed the test for being a pilot in 1963. Later I took yet another course, in the Canal Zone in Panama. After that I was an instructor. I also successfully completed a course in parachute jumping in the Canal Zone. I am now speaking of the period around 1965. Later I was trained as a jet pilot in the U.S.—in San Antonio, Texas—and later as an instructor of jet pilots. In the early 1970s, I was transferred to the government flying organization, LANCIA, which also belonged to the Somoza family, or perhaps only in part. I remained with LANCIA until the victory of the Revolution.

But weren't you at the same time a pilot in the Air Force, in the FAN? If our information is correct, you were a captain in 1978 and were promoted to major in 1979.

Air Force pilots served LANCIA simultaneously, almost as if LANCIA were a sister organization. Our promotions depended on LANCIA, however. We also flew for the Air Force, of course, because there were always emergency situations where we had to jump in. Almost all of the pilots were used in the 1979 war. We flew regular flights to the U.S. and to other countries in Central America and also for the Air Force. This is the part I played in the 1979 war.

When did you leave Nicaragua?

I believe that it was on July 17, but I'm not entirely sure. Although there was a war, I flew passengers and freight during this time.

I think that the number of flights with passengers and freight increased considerably during this time—international as well as national flights. There were a lot of people who wanted to get all their belongings out. In mid-July I flew a DC-6 to Guatemala City. It was on July 16, with three people on board. I don't remember who flew with me. In any case, I flew as the captain. For technical reasons we had to stay overnight in Guatemala. At seven o'clock the next morning we flew back. At about 7:30 we reached Managua again. Over the radio I learned that several planes were leaving the airport just then, without having received clearance from the tower. I couldn't imagine what might be waiting for me on the ground at that moment. It didn't occur to me that all hell might be breaking loose down there.

I requested permission to land from the tower and received it immediately. I landed the plane and pulled up in front of the LANCIA hanger. There were people everywhere. Everything was extraordinarily hectic, out of control. There were civilians on the airfield, military men with their weapons drawn—everything helter-skelter. The head of the Air Force, Lieutenant Donald Frisione, came to the plane. He had just become the commander of the FAN, and I asked him what was going on. He was dazed and asked me right away which plane I could fly out again. I pointed to my DC-6. Then he said, very loudly and officially, that on the basis of his authority as commander of the FAN, all aircraft were subject to his orders, and also that all planes would be transferred immediately to Guatemala. We were supposed to take as many soldiers as the planes could hold. He had received this order from the General Staff, he said, and was just now giving it to me.

What did you do after you received this order?

I didn't ask him anything else because he cut me off with a wave of the hand. He had no time to talk with me just then, because he also had to leave and take soldiers with him. We hadn't shut off our engines yet and I gave the order to cut two of them so that passengers could board. Immediately the first passengers stormed on: military men, civilians, everyone all mixed up, about 70 people. I started the engines up because more and more people were storming the plane. We had to press through this mass of people with the engines on, to the runway.

An undescribable panic prevailed. I believe that the airfield had gone completely out of control. I estimate that between 5,000 and 6,000 people were running around there, all of them trying to get to a plane. I couldn't do anything more. There wasn't a single seat left in the plane. We had been flying freight before this. People were pressing against each other and held each other up. Even 70 people was too many, but I carried out the order I had received.

Were you even able to start amidst all this tumult?

Shortly before take-off, we were shot at with automatic pistols. I couldn't see who was shooting. Perhaps it was army personnel; as I said, everything was falling apart. Everyone just wanted to get away. Those who couldn't get a seat acted as if they were insane. They simply shot at all the planes that were taking off, the planes that hadn't taken them along. But fortunately we weren't hit and were able to take off. We flew to Tegucigalpa and landed. There were already several other Nicaraguan planes there. We pulled up on ground that belonged to the Honduran Air Force.

But you were flying a transport plane full of passengers. Why did you land on a strip belonging to the Honduran Air Force?

Those were our orders. All military or civilian planes flying out of Nicaragua were supposed to remain under military control. Those were my orders. I landed, and no one told me what was going on, what we were supposed to do. My final order was to take all the people who would fit into the plane and fly them to Tegucigalpa. That is what I did. In Tegucigalpa, we were split up according to service rank and lodged in different barracks. I stayed together with the higher-ranking officers. As you know, I was a major at this time.

Didn't you receive any new orders?

No. We were told that we would not be allowed to fly back anymore. The planes stayed there.

One day later, I think it was July 18, the Foreign Minister of Honduras visited us. I think his name was Pérez. He told us that we had to stay in Honduras. We would be treated as political refugees. As refugees we would be protected by the government of Honduras. We couldn't return to Nicaragua, and weren't allowed to use the planes anymore. This was proscribed by international agreements. But I think that was on the 19th. Yes, it was already July 19.

Now what did you, an ex-major in the FAN, do as a political exile?

We stayed in Honduras, the planes stayed in Honduras. My family— my parents, my wife and my children—were in Guatemala. Before I went to Honduras, I had already brought them to Guatemala. I therefore applied for permission to emigrate to Guatemala. They gave me a passport, everyone who wanted to go got a passport. We had no difficulties in Guatemala. Everywhere, people helped us find work. We got support and built new lives.

By whom were you supported?

By the government, directly by the government. In addition, we still had professional connections. I've worked my whole life in the flying business. So I flew the Guatemala-Miami and New Orleans route. I flew freight for a company, a sister company of AVIATECA, in a DC 6. The pay wasn't great. When I worked in Nicaragua, I earned a great deal more, about $1,600 U.S., as a flight captain. I had saved some of it, had bought several houses and pieces of land, which I still had to pay off—one in the part of the city called Las Colinas, in Managua, and one in the Colonia Independencia. I didn't have any landed property, but a bank account with, at that time, about 60,000 córdobas. Well, that wasn't a lot.

The FAN was known for giving people the opportunity to do a good business in smuggled goods. Almost all of the pilots drove big cars, usually Mercedes Benzes. It was said that the pilots were the pampered little sons of Somoza...

My background is modest. My father was a small farmer, and when he gave up farming, he busied himself with several small businesses, selling grain and so forth. I had already decided as a schoolboy to become a pilot. When we moved to the capitol, it became possible for me to pursue this profession. Naturally, it was a problem that it was damned expensive to fly. That's obvious. The only chance for me was the Air Force.

What did you do in Guatemala?

I have always worked as a pilot. But I had great obligations. I had to support my family and my parents and several brothers who were studying at the University. I didn't earn enough in Guatemala. We therefore decided to go back to Honduras. There I could fly a crop-spraying plane, which was work I had done before from time to time.

That's a pretty dangerous job. Usually only pilots who have just completed their training and need a job do that.

Yes, that's true. But because I had these obligations and because I had worked with insecticides before, I wasn't afraid of it. This work put me in the black. I only flew part of the time, though; let's say six months out of the year. During the rest of the year, I flew commercial planes in Guatemala. So I was able to keep my head above water and keep the financial problems of the family under control. I did this until 1983.

What happened to your military friends?

I had ongoing contact with the people who were building the counterrevolution at that time. It couldn't be avoided, simply because of the scope of the National Guard.

I estimate that the National Guard had about 5,000 active members. The Air Force, however, was relatively small with about 600 members.

The Air Force was always poorly organized. As a member of the Air Force, you weren't supposed to have any connections with a civilian flying company. But it was always done. As I said, I worked with insecticides, spraying in Honduras and also in Guatemala.

Who decided to build up a new air force for the counterrevolution? How did they come into contact with you?

I still hadn't been contacted in 1982. It wasn't until a year later that I really joined in. I was working outside Tegucigalpa, in a rural region. Only when I came into the city did I see several of my old comrades. One belonged to the FDN, that went without saying. But we didn't yet meet in an organized way. I don't know whether they already had planes at that time or whether there had been any flights. I honestly don't know. Of course I was occasionally approached, and we talked about flying. I was also told that we would soon have a new air force, and I was asked whether I was still prepared to take part in the liberation of Nicaragua. I told them that they could count on me if that became necessary. Lieutenant Gómez, who commanded the FDN air force, was in Honduras at this time. We knew each other from before. I also knew Lieutenant Bermúdez. Because the Air Force [of Somoza] was so small, almost all of the officers knew each other. They reported to me on the situation and gave me information about what was going on in Nicaragua. In Honduras, films were constantly being shown on television about Nicaragua. We could see how the people were fleeing Nicaragua because of the Communist regime that the Sandinistas had set up.

Were the television films in Honduras enough for you to form an opinion of what was really happening in Nicaragua?

No, I wasn't sure what was really going on in Nicaragua. I wasn't there! In order to be really sure, you'd have to be in Nicaragua yourself. I had been out of the country the whole time. But I was sure that the people were not satisfied with the present government, and I was also sure that I had to take a stand.

Weren't you affiliated with a party during the time of Somoza?

Yes, of course, but *Somocismo* was a thing of the past. Let me put it this way: there was my family, all of them Nicaraguans. They should be able to live in Nicaragua again. We were in exile, and at that time there had been no indication by the Sandinista government, no possibility, that we would be able to go home and start living our lives again as we were used to—a completely normal life. So I thought that the only possible hope of returning to Nicaragua would be by fighting for it.

When I joined up with the FDN, I was the only pilot besides Major Gómez, who had been with them for a long time. I had just moved to the U.S. at that time and wanted to get a new start there. I was already working when they informed me that they now had a transport plane, for supporting the operations of the Task Forces, and that even more Task Forces would be operating in Nicaragua. It appeared that there would soon be more airplanes and helicopters. In May, 1983 I arrived from Miami, and they really did have a C47. I had had years of experience with this plane, of course. I began to work with it when everything was clear. This plane was under the command of Captain Hugo Aguilar Méndez. He died shortly after our crash here.

What do you mean by "when everything was clear?" And what is a C47?

At the Aguacate base in Catama, in the department of Olacho

in Honduras, the runway had pretty much gone to ruin. We began to rebuild it, and then the air force was installed there. You aren't familiar with the C47? It is a military version of the DC4. They are almost exactly the same. The only thing that distinguishes them is the freight door—it is much larger than normal. That was my plane. When everything was ready, we only had two planes. I was then promoted to deputy commander and was responsible for operations based at our airfield. When I was shot down, I had over 10,000 hours in the air behind me.

It isn't clear to me how a pilot with 10,000 hours of experience could get into such an adventure. How could your flight have been safe? Were you getting logistical support from the U.S. at this time?

I can't characterize it as an adventure—rather, I was convinced that it was my responsibility to oppose what had been done to Nicaragua. I am an expert at responsibility. Yes, I am that, and I had to carry out this new assignment. It was apparent that it was dangerous. That's why I'm sitting here, and part of the crew is dead. I want to emphasize once again—it was no adventure for me, but rather a personal duty which I accepted for my people. For this reason I had to do this job, as an expert, as well as possible.

How did you do this job?

We worked closely with the Task Forces. They informed the staff directly of their positions. The staff, through Comandante Gómez, gave me my coordinates, where the Task Force was located. Based on this, I formulated a plan, analyzed the situation, made a flight plan. Then we loaded the freight into the plane and unloaded it over the agreed-upon drop point. After that we immediately headed home to the base. We loaded a great variety of things. I participated in only two flights—on the third, I was shot down.

Only two flights? During what time periods?

Of course, we made a great many flights, but for the most

part the coordinates weren't right and we didn't find the drop point. We maintained contact via radio. The Task Force would then display a visible signal which had been agreed on. It could be a particular smoke signal or certain panels with bright colors, red or orange, which they laid together to make a particular symbol.

After your last flight, 70,000 rounds of ammunition for FAL rifles, 300 M79 grenades, two machine guns, Brownings, equipment, boxes of medicine, backpacks, even boots were found in your plane.

When we received the freight, it had already been packed to take along on a particular flight. We didn't know what was in the freight that we flew. You can believe me about that. We were only interested in the total weight and the bulk of the goods, because of the trim—nothing else. We took on between 4,000 and 5,000 pounds. Often medicine, but also munitions. I still don't know what was on board when we were shot down. Afterward, I learned for the first time that we had boots and medicine and other things. My responsibility was to bring this freight to a particular point. That was what I had to do, nothing more. That is, of course, clear. In all military organizations throughout the world, and particularly in the situation in which we found ourselves, there is always a division of responsibility between action and information. Everything is divided up, in every imaginable situation. That was what I knew, and that was all. The air freight came to us at the Aguacate base in trucks. We had only a normal-sized runway there, which was relatively small. It was therefore impossible to land large airplanes there. The freight arrived by land and usually arrived at night. As pilots we had nothing to do with that.

The Aguacate base is located within the operational boundaries of the Big Pine II exercises of the Honduran and U.S. armies. So it is easy to imagine where the freight came from, and who rebuilt the runway.

I simply can't say where the freight came from. I would have no reason to hide this information from you if I knew it. I had no idea where these things came from. There was one person responsible for the depot, who received the freight, and another person was responsible for preparing the freight in accordance with our cargo capacity. I then received a copy of a form with the weight information. It was my duty, as I have just said, to fly the freight into the Nicaraguan interior. I flew where there was someone who received the freight and then distributed it. Of course, you are assuming that I knew where all these things came from. But I would certainly tell you if I knew, even if that might cause problems.

When you flew supplies in your C47 to the Task Force—which was led by a former first-lieutenant of the EEBI, José Francisco Ruiz Castellanos, "Renato"—you were hit by anti-aircraft fire. Two of those on board, former National Guardsman Wilfredo Malot and the man responsible for dropping the freight, known as "Waslala," parachuted out. What happened when you were hit?

The plane caught fire, it was badly hit, and the left engine began to burn. The cabin was full of dense smoke in a split second. We couldn't see anything anymore. I didn't notice that several men had parachuted out. We lost power, and the only patch of land that was available for an emergency landing looked from above like a small empty hill. When we were down lower, I saw that it was a harvested corn field. We decided to land there and got ready for an emergency landing so that at least the plane wouldn't catch fire from below. We lowered our speed to 60 knots and didn't use the hydraulic gears. The landing was violent. The plane flew apart into two or three pieces. Several men were badly injured. But fortunately we didn't catch fire.

We first had to get a grip on things. Two men were unconscious. They later died of their injuries. Both of my co-pilot's legs were broken. There was a total of seven of us in the plane—two pilots, a mechanic, and four freight men, "kickers" as the Americans call them. We thought about what to do. It was clear to us, or rather, to those of us who were conscious, that we couldn't help those who were unconscious. We couldn't even hide them. The mechanic and I remained behind. I had trained him, had shown him how to throw out freight at the right moment. As I've already said, I had also completed a course in parachute jumping. I had jumped seven times and also have a good idea of how to divide up freight on a plane, how to attach it to a parachute, and also how to jump with it.

We estimated that the Task Force wasn't far away. But I no longer remember how long it took before a *miliciano* came and after him more men, not *milicianos* but farmers, who threatened us with weapons. They held us with cocked rifles. We didn't attempt any sort of resistance, and told them that we had wounded men. We asked them to help us, and they did help us then.

It had been understood, of course, that we could be shot down at any time, but we thought we would be shot down by planes. They have jet-fighters here, you know. Bringing down a C47 is child's play. We flew so that no fighter planes would see us. The C47 is a very slow plane. We didn't think that they would bring us down with anti-aircraft guns, though. It must have been an anti-aircraft rocket, with a nose that reacts to heat waves. First our left engine flew apart. Shortly before we reached the drop point, I thought that the Task Force would secure the area for us, since we had to descend to an altitude of 400 feet to make the drop. It was at this altitude that we were hit. You need that low an altitude to make a drop accurately. If you fly higher, the freight could be carried away by the wind or be lost in the forest. As I said, I was rather surprised to be hit there by anti-aircraft fire. I was sure that we would be appropriately covered at our drop point. I have never seen "Renato," and I don't know him either, but it was clear that the freight was for him.

The farmers subsequently reported that you lied. You told them that you were flying for the Sandinista Air Force, for Commander Modesto Rojas, who is responsible for this zone, although you wore the bluish-green uniforms of the FDN.

When we were taken prisoner, I thought to myself that we would be summarily shot, right next to the plane. I thought that the farmers wouldn't have the least idea of who we were. So I simply said that we were from the Sandinista Air Force. I did that for two reasons: our Task Force couldn't have been very far away and might attack. We therefore had to play for time. Perhaps, too, some sort of lucky coincidence would happen, and we would escape from this situation. That is why, and I must say that I was initially successful, I simply lied to them. They believed me at first. They didn't know who we were or that it was an FDN plane. They only asked us what we were doing there. That is why I told them we were with the Sandinista Air Force.

You said before that you had two houses. Were they expropriated?

I don't know. I left and I don't know what has happened to them.

What happened to the rest of your property?

I don't know, I haven't paid any attention to that, either.

I can't understand that. A man invests a huge amount of money in the purchase of two large homes, makes an effort to get his family and perhaps his money as well out of the country, and then ceases to concern himself with his possessions, with his financial affairs.

I discovered that trials were being held. All of those connected with the armed forces were being expropriated. I assumed that I was included. I haven't thought about it much beyond that. I will only be able to clarify all of that when we return, when we begin to work here again.

As deputy commander of the FDN Air Force, didn't you earn

$1,500 U.S. a month?

I must insist that I received no money, no payment of any kind.

Then how did you support your family? You said before that your primary concern was the financial security of your family.

That goes without saying. When I was still working with the crop-spraying planes in Guatemala, I talked to Major Gómez and Major Bermúdez about what kind of support they would be able to give my family if I were to fly for the FDN. The figure was much lower than what I was earning at the time. They didn't pay me a commission, but rather a subsidy for my family. I had earned a lot more previously. When I began making the flights to Nicaragua, they made it clear to me that they would in no way be able to give me what I had been earning before, or pay me what my work was really worth. They could only give me a subsidy.

Your duty was to supply the Task Forces from the air. What was the significance of those flights?

The goal was the liberation of Nicaragua. The replacement of the present government with a government formed through free elections, and the creation of an army which is totally separated from politics, an apolitical army.

What would happen to the reforms of the Sandinistas?

I don't know anything about that, that is for the politicians to decide. I was a member of the military, the Air Force. I can't comment on anything else. I don't know what the politicians of the FDN have in mind.

So it was simply the idea of liberating your country that inspired you to put your skills to use?

Yes, exactly, that's precisely it.

And all that because you saw several films on Honduran television and got some other information. That is hard to believe in the case of someone with your analytical skills.

It's a combination of a lot of things. It was not only the films that I saw, but also my own conversations with many friends and acquaintances who had left Nicaragua and whose possessions were totally confiscated. I spoke with them not only in Honduras, but also in Guatemala, in the U.S., everywhere I went. I believe that it is my duty as a Nicaraguan and a person loyal to my homeland to give up everything for freedom and to do it at any time. For this reason I thought that what I did was right.

And what do you think now?

I was sentenced to 30 years in prison by the anti-Somocista tribunal. I have been in prison for seven months now, and I will serve out my term. I was sentenced because I acted against the government. When the members of this government were fighting against Somoza, they also received harsh sentences. I'm not complaining about the treatment I've received in prison. I haven't been tortured by the security forces, nor did they torture me when I was taken prisoner. Yes, I must say that I have been properly treated. Quite differently from what I had expected. I stand behind what I did. Every human being has ideals. These are mine. I wanted to liberate my country from a system with which the Nicaraguan people do not agree. I thought I would do the best thing. I am convinced that fighting in this way was the only thing to do.

Leader of the contras who killed German doctor and the three nurses.

Contras at the "Las Dificultades" camp in Honduras.

Above, Comandante Edén Pastora of ARDE before his troops on the Río San Juan. Below, ARDE unit on the Río San Juan.

Members of the FDN General Staff (from left): Argentine adviser Santiago Villegas;
Tomás Martínez, Comandante "Tito"; Emilio Echaverry, Director of the General Staff,
"El Fierro"; Pedro Ortiz Centeno, Comandante "El Suicida"; Comandante "Atila."

Comandante
"Mac," FDN,
Nicarao Base,
May 1983,
northern
Nicaragua.

Miskito training with an M-60 at contra camp.

New FDN recruits.

Above, William Baltodano Herrera. Below, Pedro Javier Núñez Cabezas.

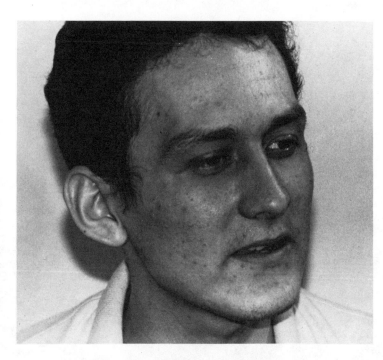

Ocotal, Nicaragua, after contra attack of January 1, 1984. Above, office of the INE (energy agency). Below, office of the Ministry of Agrarian Reform, "Programs for Farmers."

"Our Basic Training Was in Guerrilla Warfare and Sabotage"
Conversation with Emerson Uriel Navarrete Medrano

My name is Emerson Uriel Navarrete. I come from Chinandega or, more precisely, from Cosmapa. I am 29 years old. I worked for the state security service in Chinandega, but nothing exciting happened. The Sandinistas did not come that far, and there were no heavy battles, no battles at all. I had a really quiet job. On June 18, 1979, we heard on the radio that it would be better to pull back, for tactical reasons. There was no more ammunition, so we could not continue to fight without great losses. Therefore, a general retreat would be best. Everybody should try to get out of the country as fast as possible, preferably to Honduras. If the Guardia is running away, I thought, then it's really time to go. We got a boat with an outboard motor and took off.

And where did you find a boat so quickly??

In Puerto Morazún, which is a little harbor on an inlet leading to the Gulf of Fonseca. From there we went to the island of El Guapinol and from there to a small Honduran harbor. I don't remember the name of it any more.

How many of you were in the boat?

There were 18 of us, all old friends who do not give up easily. We did not stay long in Honduras, but continued on to El Salvador quickly. During three years there, I studied agronomy and the fishing business, with some interruptions.

How did you get in contact with the FDN?

Through friends. We all know each other, and in El Salvador there are a lot of old buddies. They told me what was happening and that they had taken up arms to fight the new regime. They explained that it would benefit me to join them and besides, it was my duty as an old comrade to take part in this struggle.

And when did you decide to go with them?

It was in April, 1982 that I decided to join. I went to the "Sagitario" training camp, which was commanded by "El Suicida" at that time.

What kind of military training did you have before this?

I was a trained soldier. At the camp I was trained as a specialist in guerrilla warfare, in sabotage. That was all.

Before the 19th of July, when you were working for state security, had you killed anybody?

No. Not privately. In the military, of course, I did. Several. That was military duty. You had to do it, not because you liked it but because it was an order.

Now you specialized more. What for?

I learned how to blow up bridges, how to plan blowing up industrial plants, how to sabotage strategic buildings.

How long did you stay in the camp?

A month, a little more than a month. The camp is in the Minas Caramuyo region.

Besides the training, what did you do at the camp?

We had a good life, really. We had enough to eat, played baseball on the landing field. We played cards, everything men enjoy.

How many persons are usually in the training camp?

About 700, sometimes more, sometimes less.

Who provided the necessities for such a large group? Where did the food come from?

The cattle mostly came from Nicaragua. There were special units that had to procure meat from Nicaragua. They stole cattle from the pastures of INRA, the Agrarian Reform department of the Nicaraguan government. At least that's how it was in April 1982, when you still had to buy cloth, beans, and corn with your own money.

And what about the weapons?

We already had the FAL and M-14; later the heavier weapons arrived. But I'm not sure about this, because I had left the camp before that. I was ordered to Nicaragua, to be a security guard for newly recruited peasants who were on the road to Honduras. There were about 500 civilians—farmers—who were to replenish our troops, and to whom we gave an escort. We were a small group of 12, but there were about 200 men who removed the people from their villages. That means there were 200 of us, armed, to remove 500 farmers from their villages. When I got back to Honduras, I received an order to go to El Salvador. They needed me there for a special assignment.

Why did they choose you in particular for this task?

I'm sure it was because I knew El Salvador pretty well from when I studied there.

But there are a lot of other people who know El Salvador well.

Perhaps they did not have the right training.

Training for what?

Our basic training was in guerrilla warfare and sabotage. Almost all the people in our group were from the military, ex-National Guards. There were also a lawyer and two physicians. Four in our group had academic titles.

How did you get to El Salvador?

On foot, through the woods. We also had to get across a river, but immediately beyond that was the border. We wore civilian clothes, entirely inconspicuous. We did not have papers, no one in authority guided us.

How did you know where you could cross safely? Did you get particular instructions?

They just took us to a certain place and showed us what direction to go in. We got enough money to pay for transportation.

Did anything happen when you crossed the border?

Nothing. Nothing at all. Our crossing was entirely normal, there were no soldiers to be seen. We went on and arrived at a small border village, La Unión.

How did that go?

We made friends with the secretary of the mayor. A friend of ours, also Nicaraguan, invited the secretary over, and when he was drunk we offered him money. He immediately gave us personal papers. They were blank. One of us, who had good handwriting, wrote our names on the papers. The papers were stamped. They were perfect. The names were ours, only they showed us as having Salvadoran birthplaces and, at the end, we forged the mayor's signature.

The stamps were official?

Yes. Also, the signature of the secretary was real. The only signature we had to forge was the mayor's. He just wasn't there and could not sign the papers. Without those falsified papers, it would have been impossible to get to San Salvador. I really did a good job with my personal papers. Several times on the way to San Salvador, they took us off the bus, all of us. We had to put our hands up against the bus, and they searched us for weapons. They also demanded to see our papers, and they were satisfied with them. In San Salvador we managed to get tax receipts to go with our personal papers. You also have to show tax receipts continuously.

How did you meet your contact?

We were told to go to the police department, to see a Major Stabin. This we did, immediately—not the whole group of 12, of course, but two at a time. He was the right person. He ordered a car to take us to the Hotel Alameda in the center of the city. We rested there until we were called to a meeting, where we were informed that we were to work for several businessmen. They let us wait two days. During those days, we did nothing, nothing at all. We strolled around, went to the movies, to McDonald's. Only five in our group knew San Salvador, so we showed the others the city. Then the businessmen came to the hotel and decided who we would each work for. Immediately after the meeting everybody left with his new boss.

Who were the new bosses?

Salvadoran big businessmen, people from the elite families: Piojil, Goirola, Palomo, Melicar. Those are the most important names. They have the money. It is said that 14 families decide what is done, and we worked for some of them.

What were your duties?

We were bodyguards. We were always with them, at the office, at home, in the city—we stuck to them like burrs. These people really live in danger. Once, when I was inside the house, a bomb exploded only 20 meters away. Half the house flew into the air, as well as two cars. If you have to live like that, naturally you are interested in good protection. Above all, they fear being kidnapped and having impossible amounts of money demanded from their families.

How were these families connected to the FDN?

I can't say. I only know that the FDN sent us to El Salvador to work for these families.

How long did you do that?

I worked as a bodyguard in El Salvador for over a year. Some of our group remained there. I was called back to Honduras, because I was needed. They wanted people like me to train for special assignments

How did you leave El Salvador this time?

This time by boat, to the harbor of San Lorenzo. In Tegucigalpa I was told to take a new training course. First I stayed a while at the camp in Las Vegas, then I was moved to Roatán, which was commanded by somebody named Andrés.

What kind of special training were you to take?

Guerrilla warfare again, but also training in special kinds of marine work, sabotage, and for special tasks. Basically it was special training in sabotage, how to attack targets from piranha boats [a type of speedboat]. We practiced target-shooting on barrels and tires, how to attach underwater explosives, how to lay underwater mines. We learned diving with and without oxygen tanks, piloting speedboats, survival techniques, especially surviving at sea without food, even how to survive if you have nothing to eat or to drink. I already knew how to handle bombs, but of course these things function somewhat differently under water. They have different timing devices, different clock-works.

You just told me that you knew how to handle bombs...

Yes, that we learned at the Sagitario camp—how to position bombs, how to place mines on the ground—of course, all this is part of basic training. Now we had to learn how to do that in the water. We had to learn how to handle oxygen tanks.

Were you already able to dive?

No, and we only practiced three times in the swimming pool, then we immediately went out into the open seas. In the open sea, it becomes serious. That is the best training.

*In other words, you specialized in marine sabotage, frogman
actions. What interests me is, how can you be sure to hit a target
from a piranha?*

The boats are terribly fast, but also heavy. Besides three
cylinders, which means 800 liters of gasoline, there is a special
valve system to stabilize yourself in the water. You take in more
water if the speed increases, to get more stability.

Therefore you lay fairly deep in the water?

Yes, that's the trick, so you will not have so many problems
with the waves. At maximum speed, the boats are so heavy that
they would sink immediately if the motor stopped. Only this special system prevents that. If you slow down, the water will be
pumped out of the boat.

How many people can get in one boat?

From four to six. It depends on the weight you carry with you.
The boat is equipped with three machine-guns, two on both sides
of the back and one in front, in the middle. They are either M-60
or M-50, it depends.

Did you practice shooting?

Yes, we prepared the boat for combat, filled it with gasoline,
and then we took off. Our target was about one to one-and-a-half
kilometers away.

Were you trained in a school or in a barracks?

It was a training center on the island of Roatán.

How many boats were there to use in the training?

I only knew about the boats that belonged directly to the school,
that were stationed there. We were a long way from the village.

How many persons took this training and how long did it last?

It was an intensive course. It lasted exactly one month. We
got up at 4 a.m.; at 5 a.m. the calisthenics started and lasted until

6 or 6:30. After that we had breakfast, and then the training began. There were ten of us.

Who were the other nine who took the course?

All Nicaraguans.

How were they selected?

It was a colorful crowd. Some were university graduates, some were farmers from the coastal area, who were illiterate.

Who determined the selection?

Everybody had to have been noticed, and everybody had to get along with the officers.

Did you also learn to pilot a speedboat?

Everybody had to learn this, because nobody knows what will happen in an attack. The boats were very powerful. They had two motors of either 275 hp or 350 hp each, a total of 700 hp. They were great, those boats.

Who were the teachers? Where did they come from?

They were North Americans. They did not speak perfect Spanish, but they tried hard.

Did the teachers live together with you in the camp?

No, they arrived at the training punctually and afterwards they disappeared immediately. They gave us specific instructions as to what we had to do in the exercises. Then they evaluated what we had done, right or wrong, in a very precise way.

Did you also get survival training?

Yes, of course. If a mission lasts three days, it's possible that the engines would quit and you would be left floating on the open sea. That happened once, when we were ordered to head in the direction of Nicaragua to attack a certain target. Suddenly we realized, after five or six hours, that the engine was not working right. We turned them all off, and none of them worked again. If you

have a heavily loaded boat, you cannot carry reserve-batteries
with you. We had to try to find the problem in the electrical system. It could also happen that we would realize after some hours
at sea that the gasoline had run out. Of course, we had oars with
us, but they are only useful to find out if there is a current that
you can use. These were the jokes they played on us. Often they
put used spark plugs in the motor, which was very dangerous if
the motor stopped and the water could not be pumped out. If we
did not realize the mistake in time—that happened several times—
we could only drift at sea. It lasted one or two days until they
picked us up. We didn't have anything to eat and our lips cracked
because they were so dry.

Why didn't you have enough food in the boat?

I don't know. It's crazy. But they told us there wasn't enough
space.

Didn't you sometimes think about the risk?

No, not really. These were such expensive boats that we were
sure they would pick us up.

Didn't you have a wireless in the boat?

Sure, but there were also times when they just made a mistake in the transmitter. Then we only had our walkie-talkies to
depend on.

Is there radar on the boats, or how do you find your way at night?

These are sophisticated boats. They have radar systems, sonar
systems, automatic pilots, everything that modern technology
offers today. Close to the little steering wheel is the radar screen.
The boat radar was very precise. We could find a medium-sized
piece of wood from a distance of four kilometers.

Did you make a real attack by boat?

No, we only practiced how to make such an attack.

Tell us again precisely where the school is.

On the island of Roatán, entirely isolated. We had no contact with the people there. In fact we didn't even see who the house-keeper was. We only left the school for training.

Did you have contact with your instructors?

Only during instruction. Of course, we tried to talk to them after the training, but usually they left immediately. They had a special recreation room. They determined what we had to do, whether we had breakfast or dinner, whether we were allowed to go swimming or if an action was planned. They gave orders that so many persons should go in one boat and so many in the other one.

Did you lay mines during your training?

No. This was not part of our training. We only learned to han-dle explosives underwater. For example, we got a map on which the object we were to destroy was marked. We calculated how far it was, then tried to locate it with our radar. We usually found the object immediately. Then we jumped into the water, dived to the object, and attached the explosives to it. We had to escape fast, because it would explode automatically. We waited until the explosion occurred and dived again to see if we had really des-troyed the object. Usually the explosive was so strong that noth-ing was left.

Was there rank inside the group?

No. We all had the same grade, everybody was responsible for his assignment, everybody had to know the same and be able to do the same.

And after the course was over?

We went back to the Las Vegas camp, to wait for orders to attack.

How did you leave the island?

A FDN helicopter carried us to Tegucigalpa and from there

via Las Vegas to Catacama. Catacama is really just a camp with a landing strip. From there we were moved to the El Aguacate camp. After a short rest we came to the Bocay camp, directly on the Nicaraguan border.

It seems to me somewhat contradictory: you were trained for the piranhas and then ordered to a guerrilla unit in the mountains.

That's because we had a little problem. We all did well in the exam, and were happy to have finished the hard training. Then we had a day off and hung around the recreation room. There were some cartons of beer, and of course we got drunk. So we started to slander God and the whole world, saying that we did not like certain things, and we also mentioned names. I myself was very reserved, but some of the farmers said they were not enthusiastic about continuing. Our talk was secretly overheard. Before this we had been told we would stay with the navy, but after listening to our talk, they put us under arrest for one day. All of us. The result was that we were sent to different battle units. They told us that with people like us, they could not risk going ahead with the attacks for which we had been chosen. They did not trust the group anymore, because nobody could be sure what would happen if someone was alone in a boat during an attack.

Which unit did you belong to, in San José de Bocay on the Nicaraguan border?

I was in the unit commanded by "Policeman López." Its name was the San Jacinto Battle Unit. Everything was prepared for the invasion of Nicaragua. There were about 100 of us, and we were to cross the border in June 1983.

If I am right, that was the camp led by "Renato."

Yes, that's right. First it was under "Policeman López," who was called back to Tegucigalpa, and then Comandante "Renato" took over the leadership. We badly needed new people, so we went into Nicaragua several times to recruit farmers, take them to Honduras, train them, and integrate them into the battle units.

How long were you in "Renato's" camp?

Not very long. We left on June 14 to hurry to Chontales and Boaco, in central Nicaragua.

To Boaco, that means deep inside of Nicaragua?

Our group advanced the farthest into Nicaragua. We crossed the Río Coco. The Sumus, Indians who live there, helped us over the river with their canoes. It took about two days for all of us to cross the river.

Didn't you run into Sandinista troops on your march after that?

No, there was nobody, it was pure jungle. It isn't easy to find anybody in the area of San Andrés de Bocay. The same for San José de Bocay, Amaca, and Amaquita. We could do what we wanted there.

What happened after this?

Close to Mateplátano, Comandante "Renato" met his officers and about 100 people. After this we lost sight of them. We were then a unit of 140 soldiers. The rest were lost in some way. On the radio we heard they had gone back to Honduras. We couldn't wait for them. It was decided they should slip into Nicaragua with another unit. We crossed the main road and reached Tijeria. On the way, new people constantly joined us.

Wasn't it an important part of "Plan C" to set up roadblocks and ambushes?

We didn't set up any roadblocks. Our job was to head for Boaco and Chontales directly, if possible without engaging in combat. Of course we often had the opportunity to set an ambush, but that wasn't our job.

How was food provided for 140 persons on the march?

In that area, there are a lot of cattle that nobody owns. The peasants are not there anymore. They have escaped or died. You can round up the cattle and kill them. We were never hungry, we always had enough food. During this time we did not yet receive goods via air-transport.

What weapons did you have?

FAL guns. Everybody carried 700 bullets, a weight of about 25 kilograms. That's damned heavy. The first and the second day, you think your back will break, but after that, you get used to it. The fifth day you don't feel it anymore.

How far did you get?

Close to Chontales—about 11 kilometers from there, between Cuapa and Boaco.

When was that?

From Honduras to Chontales is about 300 kilometers as the crow flies. If you allow for the actual route, it's nearly double. We started on June 14 and arrived at the beginning of September.

Without any battles?

Yes. I already told you. We marched 30 to 35 kilometers when necessary, from 6 a.m. until 7 p.m. Then we hid.

Were there women with you?

Of course, we had a lot of women with us. They were armed like men, carried FAL guns and the same backpacks. In fact, I believe the women were much stronger than we were. Men often go crazy after a day-long march in the bright sun, and become feverish. No one has any desire to do anything. You just want to sit down. Often the women then take the men's backpacks and carry them on their heads—in addition to all their own stuff, of course. You only have to carry your gun, the women carry all the other things. After five kilometers you will be recovered to the extent that you are able to carry your own stuff again. As I told you, many things worked out well only because we had so many women with us.

There really were no battles during this long march?

Only once. At the little village of Huasayamar, we met 200 soldiers of the Sandinista army. They fired for a little bit and then escaped. . . . We rested there for two days and then marched further into the hills. A helicopter of the Sandinista Air Force followed us. They fired at us with a machine-gun, but they didn't hit us; the woods saved us.

What did you do when you arrived in the villages?

First we were only concerned with the people working for the state, for the Agrarian Reform department and the other divisions. Mostly we forced them to come with us. Of course we used violence. The only ones who sometimes joined us without force were peasants. To the people working for the government, you first have to read them a lesson. We loaded all the stuff on their shoulders, all the things we carried with us, so we could move more easily.

Why did you march across Nicaragua to Boaco and Chontales?

Why indeed? To attack Boaco and Chontales, to destroy them. That was the zone where Comandante "Renato" operated. He was there in 1982, and in 1984 he wanted to start the same action.

How strong was your group by that time?

By this time, we had grown to about 250, 290, almost 300. Fortunately, each of us had taken two guns when we left Honduras, so we were able to arm all these people. Also, there were some hidden caches of weapons along the way which we emptied out, so we were able to arm the troops well. The peasants who wanted to work with us were indoctrinated politically for two days. They had to understand what they were fighting for. After this they got their guns.

What arguments did you use?

At 3 or 4 in the afternoon, when we stopped marching, the political cadre called the peasants together and talked to them.

They explained to them what Sandinismo is about, what Communism would mean to Nicaragua. That they had to fight against this. That there would be real freedom in Nicaragua only if the FSLN were tossed out of the saddle. Only then could a democracy be built, without political prisoners.

For what reasons do the peasants join the FDN?

The reasons are totally clear. First, the FDN passes through the village, and if you don't go with them, the Sandinista troops come and capture you because you have been helpful to the FDN. That you can probably handle once, but not a second time. If you didn't go with the FDN troops, then surely they left you there to cooperate with the contras.

Do you mean to say that most of the peasants go with the FDN because they are afraid of having problems with the Sandinista army?

At least, that's what I was told. The Sandinista army arrives and insults the peasants: the contras have passed through, and you must have given food to them. That is what many peasants told me. So they join us, and we try to indoctrinate them politically.

What does the FDN say about agrarian reform, literacy campaigns, and medical aid?

That's very easy. You only need to explain to the peasants that during the Somoza government they earned 15 córdobas. With 15 córdobas, one could buy 10 batteries for a small radio at that time. Today they probably earn 40 córdobas, but one cannot get a single battery with that. Before, they bought 20 pounds of rice with 15 córdobas. Today, they can buy only 2 pounds with 40 córdobas. It is so expensive because the Sandinistas send all the rice to the U.S.S.R. and to Cuba. That's how we explain it to them. In former times, they had it bad, but they were well-off. Today they are better off, but things are worse for them. You know as well as I do that a peasant has nothing in his head but straw. He doesn't think about things the way that somebody who went to school does. Two or three stories well-told, and he will join you.

Do the new recruits get a uniform?

Not immediately. It usually takes five to seven days, after they are politically indoctrinated and can be trusted. Then they get a uniform and a gun.

I would imagine that these peasants are nothing more than cannon fodder.

Nonsense. We protect them. They march in the middle or at the rear. The units are divided into three or four groups. In a unit of 400, for example, this would be about a hundred in each group. The peasants are in a group marching in the middle of the column. The trained soldiers take care of them, so they don't suddenly become afraid if something happens.

How far is it between the groups?

Depending on the terrain, between 1 and 500 meters. This formation is tested; if one group is attacked, the other will retreat and try to circle around the attacker. Then they fire with everything they have, so that the enemy has no idea how many people there are. The others join the circle and usually we are able to encircle the enemy within a short time.

Tell us what happened at Boaco.

We had been pursued for days, and near Boaco the battle began. It was between 7 and 7:30 a.m. We had already marched a couple of hours when we realized that they were behind us. We thought we would have a strategic advantage if we could leave them far behind while some spies kept us continually informed via radio. We tried to find an opportunity to set an ambush. In the first encounter, only one of us was wounded. It was only a scratch. It's hard to say whether there were casualties, because everybody was shooting like crazy. Nobody looks around, everybody tries to save their own skin. Only the first ones, who set the trap, shot directly at the enemy. The rest were just firing as hard as they could. As I mentioned, in an ambush, the first bullets really count—because of the surprise factor. You need time to place the machine guns so you can direct your fire at the expected target. Then, when it all starts happening, the front-lines disappear and you have to fire as much as you can in order to kill everyone as fast as possible.

This ambush was set by your unit?

We were pursued by two battalions. The "Simón Bolívar" BLI (Battalion for Guerrilla Battle) and the other, I believe it was the "José Dolores Estrada" BLI, are elite units of the Sandinista army. The trap was set for the "José Dolores" Battalion. Then we retreated quickly across the river, which seemed a good place to set a new ambush.

What actually happened in this ambush?

Nothing, we only had one wounded, and he was not even badly hurt. At night, when an FDN helicopter came to supply us with ammunition and weapons, it took the wounded man. The next day I escorted 25 peasants who were new and had to be protected in case of an attack. Suddenly we were attacked and one peasant was fatally wounded. This is always a critical situation, because all the others become terrified. They then behave strangely. They throw themselves down on the ground and can't lift their heads; they put both hands over their ears. I believe they are terribly frightened. They lie with their faces in the dirt and try to bury their heads under the soil, not wanting to see or hear anything.

But surely they are armed?

Most of them, for sure, but not all. We do not have enough weapons to give to everyone. Of those who were under my protection, only one was armed; the others were not. Therefore, I had to protect them. We had to hurry and find the other unit, so they could defend us. This unit was able to welcome the pursuing army with plenty of fireworks, so they were able to defend us. In front of us, maybe 100 meters in front, there was another group of peasants. We had fallen somewhat behind because of the man who died. We slid down a steep hill and suddenly stood on a path. About 60 meters away, a woman marched at the end of another group of peasants that was in front of us. The three who slid down the hill with me to the path were armed. The woman suddenly turned around and looked back at us, saw uniforms, and thought we were Sandinista soldiers. She let loose a full magazine from her FAL. One was killed immediately, the other badly wounded.

She hit all four?

Sure. She really let loose. She thought we were Sandinistas. Because the battle was raging only a little ways back, she thought we were an advance unit. She really didn't have a chance to think about the situation and to identify us. If one is attacked there is no time to consider. All you can do is shoot first and later find out if it was the right thing to do.

Did you know the woman?

She is called Chaparra, "the little one." She is a peasant from Quilinguas and has been fighting for the FDN for three years. We lay there badly wounded until someone found us, and that was the Sandinistas. They transported the three of us first to Río Blanco and from there to Matagalpa. We lay there the whole time, because our unit did not come back to get us. We did not have a radio. The radio was carried by someone far ahead of us. If you can't communicate anymore, you either have to be able to move or you are in trouble. Without a radio you cannot call for help. You can't say where you are. One of the badly wounded died during that same night. The attack had started in the early morning and lasted until 9. When we realized that the Sandinistas were coming, we used all the ammunition we had. It's over quickly if you only have three guns. I looked in my magazine, and only had two shots left. The first I wasted. With the last one it became serious. I put the gun on my chin, here, where it is weak, between this bone, and fired.

Why did you do that?

The political cadre always told us, the torture of the Sandinistas would be terribly hard to withstand. They told us, for example, that one would be locked in a room, then a kind of press would descend from above and sharp iron spikes would come up from below, to squash you slowly.

Like a horror film. And you believed that?

Sure. I didn't know if anybody has ever seen it, but if you have once heard that could happen to you, that they slowly pull off your skin and other such jokes, then you wonder if you would be able to stand it. Being skinned alive is not my first choice. So I thought to myself that it would be better to fire a bullet through my head. Now I am sitting here, and I have to say that up to now I have not been tortured.

What was the result of the shot you fired into your chin?

It burst my jaw, went through the tongue and burst the palate, passed through the back end of my nose and went out on the left side of my nose. In all, it caused 11 fractures. I had a more beautiful nose before. Today I look like a prize fighter. Here, where the shot came out, I had two more fractures. The lower jaw won't move right anymore. Look, I can move it back and forth by hand. This certainly is the result of the detonation, because the explosion occurred practically inside my mouth. The best jaw can't stand that. I saw all my fractures on the x-rays. The teeth hung loose in my mouth. I could play on them like on the piano. The doctors put in a kind of iron wire, and now I can chew quite well again.

For a shot through the jaw with such a large caliber gun, one would think you had been to a cosmetic surgeon.

I really cannot complain. They did a good job.

You were sentenced by a court. You took part in sabotage actions and armed attacks, and killed people. These deeds are punishable by every court, regardless of what country they occur in. How can one demand amnesty for such people? Do you think that is realistic?

The Sandinistas always talk about how generous they are, and they talk about peace, and I believe that if one really wants peace, then one must begin at home. There must be a national reconciliation of the entire people. Only then is a real democracy possible. How can we have free elections if the National Guard is locked up, sentenced to 30 years in prison? That is not democracy.

After 1979, the Sandinistas set free many ex-National Guardsmen and many of them immediately joined the FDN. That seems to be your idea of democracy.

If anyone is freed through an amnesty, a general pardon, because of the generosity of the Revolution, why would he then join the armed struggle? I believe a pardon should close accounts, and life should go on.

But we have seen that many of those who were pardoned have again joined the armed struggle.

They have simply not understood what happened. They did not understand that the Revolution had pardoned them, pardoned the mistakes which they had made. Sure, there are some who will not understand why they were pardoned, and will go to fight again. Yes, the world is full of idiots, and if you are narrow-minded, you will stay that way your entire life.

"When You Don't Know the Ropes, Any Idiot Can Wrap You Around His Finger"

Conversation with Salvador Aranda Mairena

I joined the Frente [FSLN] during the last years of the struggle against Somoza. The contact was established through my two brothers, who were Sandinistas. I helped transport weapons and acted as a courier. When the uprising began in 1979, I was actively involved. I was at the takeover of the military posts at Malpaisillo, El Sauce, and Las Mojarras on the Río Grande. We captured a guy involved in the murder of Lidia Maradiaga, the union leader. We nabbed him and delivered him to our leader. I joined the United Popular Movement (MPU) in June, 1979. I helped supply people with the most necessary foods and supplies. We organized neighborhood aid. I opened a small shop and was able to help a bit. We exchanged the groceries we had for what we needed: rice for beans, flour for sugar....

Even after July 19, I remained active in the CDS (Sandinista Defense Committees). But that's when the problems began, though they were more along personal lines, I would say. Actually the revolution did me no harm, but I had personal problems with some people who had been Somoza supporters before and now played the big supporters of the revolution. Some of them were given good positions—in the UNAG (Unión Nacional de Agricultores), the CDS, and even the military. That burned me. Damn it, I had participated in the armed struggle, taken a clear position, and now

I had to watch while the same people as before skimmed the cream off the top.

In this confusion, someone came and politicized me. He made it clear to me that the revolutionary process would make everything Communist. That's what it all came down to. He told me that when you have a cow and Communism comes, the government takes your cow away. The expropriation of Somoza lands was just the beginning. Once they'd pocketed that land, then we would be next. Soon I believed it too. I owned a piece of land myself and thought that before the government takes away your land, you must oppose it. I didn't participate in the uprising to make everything Communist. I had to do something. When you have little training, cannot read or write, and don't know the ropes, then any idiot can wrap you around his finger.

So you thought the revolution had taken a turn that you had not fought for?

Exactly. That's why a representative from ARDE was able to recruit me. He convinced me that we will have a real democracy in Nicaragua when Comandante Edén Pastora takes over. That's why we must resist Communism with whatever it takes.

When was that?

That was in June 1982. After I was clear about joining the ARDE, I talked to [and recruited for ARDE] some of my old friends who had participated in the uprising. One of them was the leader of the troops in our village. He and José Mayorga and Justino Leiva joined too. These people were resolved to fight. Before long, they went to Honduras to get a month's training.

What did you tell people while recruiting them?

Actually no more than what had recruited me. That Comandante Edén Pastora had gone to Honduras, Alfonso Robelo too; that in fact all democrats who wanted nothing to do with Communism had already left the country; that we had to organize everyone to prevent the development of Communism in our country. That was the point. Naturally I also stated clearly that it would not be easy in Honduras, that you couldn't just take off. Deserters are killed. If they didn't like something about the training, then they would have to stick with it anyway. Later, when they were back here, then we could talk about it.

When the first group arrived in Honduras, there was no trace of Edén Pastora and the others we wanted to fight with. Instead there were only ex-National Guards. One month became four, and when they returned I could see for myself who the leaders were. I was really shocked. They walked across the border without any problems and came back the same way. It took them about 14 days to march back to La Mojarra. I had made camp there to receive them. They brought explosives, FALs, and carbines— everything we needed. They were specialists in sabotage, in ambushing patrols, and in acts of terror against known CDS members. They also brought along their own group leader, Charlie, an ex-National Guard. The second man was Richard. I knew him from before. We came from the same village. You have to imagine this—he was also an ex-National Guard, a real criminal type. These were supposed to be the leaders. I refused to work with such a gang. After all, I had fought under the black and red flag in the uprising against Somoza, against the Guard. How could I now fight for democracy with the Guard?

There was disagreement. Two groups formed. One went with the ex-National Guards; my people stayed with me. We decided to get in touch with our ARDE contact. When I arrived in Managua, this person was no longer there. I had to act on my own and decided to drive to Costa Rica.

Just like that, across the border to Peñas Blancas?

Naturally, but with a fake passport. I bought it from a lawyer for 1,500 córdobas. I told him I really had to get out of the country because the Sandinistas were after me. I had the passport within three days. I also obtained a visa—all without any problems. Then I went directly to Panama to re-establish contact from there. Things went smoothly in Panama. I found my contact and shortly thereafter went to Costa Rica, where I immediately went to the ARDE office in Pavas. I wanted to speak with Comandante Pastora; I wanted to fight by his side. I was questioned briefly, then I filled out a questionnaire with my name and the names of my mother, father, and children. And then they had me take the oath. When everything was OK, I was sent to Training Camp 064 near Liberia. I think this training camp was only for people of the Frente Interno, the Internal Front. In Camp 064, I had the same experience. The man in charge of training was also an ex-National Guardsman. He had even fought in the Vietnam War. I don't understand these things. I had the idea that we had to fight against a totalitarian regime, to overthrow a dictatorship. If the people don't want Communism, then they will take up weapons and overthrow the government. But here I met the same gringos, the same National Guardsmen. What was I really doing?

The training camp was technically well-equipped. It had its own communication system with the central station in San Pedro. Otherwise it was all very simple. All the supplies were located in one shack; we slept in another; a small open-sided shack was the kitchen. The camp was located on a hacienda belonging to a Cuban who occasionally dropped by and spoke with the Comandante. After about two weeks of training, we received an order over the radio to pack our things and, if possible, disappear without leaving any trace behind. The Costa Rican Civil Guard was looking for eight armed units and would certainly search the hacienda. We were quickly brought to San José, to a clandestine house in a fairly elegant district.

When was this?

This was in May 1983. And then I really found out what was going on in ARDE. One day I urgently needed a dentist. I couldn't bear the toothache any longer. They told me that they didn't have money for personal things. I had no choice but to go to a niece in San José and hit her up for money. Crazy. At the bus stop on my way back from the dentist, I just happened to see our group leader go into a luxurious nightclub with some friends. They sat in their luxurious limousines, but didn't have money to send me to the dentist. Fine, but I was on a galloping horse and had to keep riding. There was nothing I could do. Besides, I wanted to return to Nicaragua. And I did. I told them that I had people and weapons in Nicaragua, and I could accomplish much more there than I could sitting around doing nothing. They understood that.

On June 28 I crossed the border back to Nicaragua. There are some Ticos (Costa Ricans) who do a good business by bringing people across the border. They have Nicaraguans on the other side who work with them. I don't know how much it costs. They established the contact for me and took care of everything. It didn't matter to me; I only wanted to cross over. Alan was the contact. He waited for me at a certain spot in Rivas and drove me to Managua, to a country house on the road to Masaya at kilometer 14. Again my assignment was to establish contacts and form a group that could soon carry out sabotage attacks in Managua. Alan would provide the weapons. I did not have the slightest idea what it was about. That was in the hands of the leaders. We only followed their orders.

When they arrested me in the country house on August 25, I was alone. I don't know what happened to Alan. I assume that he was able to get over the border in time.

"There Was No Discipline. It Was Nothing Like a Real Army."

Conversation with Jeremías Hernández Membreño

I was born in Matiguás, in the Matagalpa district, 34 years ago. My name is Jeremías Hernández Membreño. My code name is G-20. My seven children all live in Matagalpa. I joined the FDN in August, 1982. The contact person sent me straight to Honduras and gave me some ways to get across the border, and I just set out. I crossed the border near Los Trojes and established contact with a guy called "El Turco," the Turk. I don't know his real name. "El Turco" picked me up at the border with a small car and drove me to a safe house called "El Tránsito," near Tegucigalpa. That was where I talked for the first time with 3-80, the acting military leader of the FDN.

What did you talk about?

I explained why I had come to Tegucigalpa and said I was interested in joining the FDN. The meeting was relatively formal. That same night I was handed over to a commando leader. From then on, things were very routine. I filled out a form with all my vital statistics and an oath of loyalty. That was it. Then they told me how they evaluate developments in Nicaragua, and I was suddenly one of them. Shortly afterwards I was introduced to "Benito Bravo," the leader at the La Lodosa base, who was in Tegucigalpa. That night they took me to the base, which is near the village of Las Dificultades. The next day I was amazed to see how many people were being trained at that base.

They immediately put me in military training, specializing in sabotage. This was about August 12—I can't remember the date exactly. The training lasted a total of two months. We had to get up very early. Our training began at 4 a.m., and sometimes it lasted all day, til 4 p.m.: fall down, get up, prepare ambush, operate weapons, overcome obstacles. It went like that all day. During this time we received no political training. I assume this is because the base was just being established. On October 1, 60 of us, under the command of "Rubén," set out for Nicaragua for the first time. Our assignment was to penetrate the coffee zone and sabotage the harvest that had just begun. We were told to set up road-blocks, hinder the transport of the coffee, terrorize the harvesters, and attack the ENCAFE stations where the trucks loaded with coffee leave for the drying plants. Our group could not carry out our assignment because we had a great many internal problems.

Do you mean that you were not able to fight because of these problems?

Yes, peculiar as that may sound. One evening, after 20 days on the road, we came to a farmer's house near Kilambe in the Jinotega region. We wanted a place to sleep so we could move on the next day. That night our guards stole everything in and around the house. The next day the farmer told me what had happened. I couldn't tolerate such behavior and went directly to "Rubén." I made it clear to him that I could not agree with any part of this. He searched the whole group and found the stolen things. The guilty ones did not see anything wrong with their behavior and an argument started. It stopped just short of our using our weapons on one another. The group was now split. "Rubén" wanted to punish the thieves, but they still had their weapons. That's why he let them go. Later we realized that they had taken our radio with them.

We set out, to carry out our assignment. The unit was now

directly under ''Rubén's'' command, since it had become too small
for me to act as group leader . We marched for about 40 days
and arrived in Caño Negro, 80 kilometers from Matagalpa. But
our unit had become too small to risk a battle.

About three days after the incident that had split our group,
we got into a skirmish with the Sandinista Army, and I was
wounded. We retreated, and a small group stayed with me to protect me. We had everything we needed for such situations: antibi-
otics, shots, blood-clotting medication—everything that the
gringos give their people to take along. A bullet had injured my
leg, and I could not walk. I found shelter in a house.

The people in this region help all of us—they know who we
are and what we are planning. There have been gangs in this area
operating against the government since 1980. At the end of the
month, ''Rubén'' left with a few others who had belonged to a
gang and had joined up with us. He took them along to Honduras.
Nineteen men stayed with me until my leg healed. Nothing happened the whole time, and in January I could walk again. Then
we returned to Honduras. The base camp that we had left from
no longer existed, so we went to the neighboring camp, Las
Vegas—about 30 kilometers from the border.

*At this time Plan C was in full effect. The large battle units were
already operating in Nicaragua.*

Yes, the largest battle unit, the ''Jorge Salazar,'' had started
in the Matagalpa zone. I think it was ''Tonio'' who commanded
it. We never met each other along the way, although we passed
close to each other. One unit would come in, and we would move
back out of Nicaragua. Comandante ''El Suicida'' led many battles in the region of Las Segovias and especially in the Jalapa
region. I stayed in Danlí until March so I could completely recover,
and I received daily injections. Since I no longer belonged to a
fighting unit, I stayed in a hotel.

How were you able to withdraw so easily?

You simply have to give notice, then there's no problem. After several days in Danlí I was driven by car to Tegucigalpa, to the General Staff. I reported what had happened to 3-80. He listened to my version; he had already heard "Rubén's." He promised me an investigation of these incidents and announced that there would be severe punishment in the future. Of course, I don't know what really happened. It was important to me to return to Nicaragua as soon as possible. "Wait until you're properly healed," said one, "then you can return." I drove back to my hotel and stayed there all through March, until a new fighting unit departed for Nicaragua to operate in the Molukuku area. Over a thousand people belonged to it. They gave me a special assignment. I was not under the command of the leader of this unit, and I was just supposed to travel with it into the Matagalpa region so I could report to Comandante "Tonio" there.

At that time the FDN was already using a new strategy, which was mainly implemented by the Task Forces. What duties did individual troops have?

In general, the units were now better organized, moving in groups of 60 people. These groups were spaced apart—they could be two to three hours apart. Shorter distances were naturally also possible. They communicated with good radios. I marched for two days with the fighting unit from El Cucu. At Chilamate I left them and went off in the direction of Banco del Aire, to take over the 20 people I had left behind in Winay since my injury. There were an additional 20 men under my command. I was supposed to run into "Tonio's" fighting unit, but I only found scattered groups, because the most important commanders immediately retreated to Honduras after a heavy battle. Since "Tonio" was back in Honduras, it wasn't possible to report to him.

I stayed in the Jinotega region until late April or early May. This area was under the command of "El Tigrillo," the Little Tiger, and I joined the fighting unit under his command. I was assigned to make various important roads dangerous, by setting up ambushes. There were now 60 men under my command. On our first ambush a jeep drove in, full of civilians. We shot a few rounds at the jeep and Rolando captured three people, two women and a child. For security we split into two groups about one kilometer apart. Rolando brought me the prisoners and went back to the actual ambush site. He was hardly back to his battle station when a new exchange of gunfire started, again with a civilian vehicle. The people simply did not want to surrender, and that's why he finished them off. His mistake was not shooting at the tires, but shooting directly at the vehicle. It drove on, began to skid and then landed in the ditch 200 meters further on. The driver was killed immediately, the others were seriously injured. Well, it was their own fault. I ordered Rolando to retreat for the rest of the day. But when a small truck approached, he opened fire on it. Afterwards I reprimanded Rolando and explained that there is no value in killing civilians. We had been clearly ordered to attack military vehicles only. No civilians.

What did you do with your prisoners?

In the first jeep there was a forest ranger from IRENA (the government organism that dealt with ecology), the leader of the IRENA office in this region, and a woman who was his secretary. We took the three of them along. They were under my command and I couldn't just let them go. I had to report it and await a decision from Dimas, the brother of "El Tigrillo." Dimas made no move, but ordered me over the radio to send him the prisoners.

It was clear to me what would happen, and that's why I didn't like the situation. We had attacked civilian vehicles. There were dead, seriously wounded, and prisoners. If I gave them the forest ranger, I figured they would "neutralize" him. He was the ranger for the Cerro Saslaya nature preserve. I knew him. His name was Felicito Ortiz and he tried to perform his duties the best he could. The people in the area hated him because he didn't allow the farmers to cut down trees or hunt in the park. Handing him over could mean the worst for him. In "El Tigrillo's" fighting unit, there would certainly be some people who knew him and would really enjoy paying him back. Then Pantera, one of Dimas's people, arrived with the order to send him the ranger immediately. That was an order, but I told Pantera that I expected no harm to come to this man. He took him along, and after five hours the ranger actually returned. He told me that Dimas had questioned him and then ordered him to leave. However, he was afraid because it was clear to him that they would send someone after him to kill him. He preferred to be with us again.

I hoped to hear from Dimas about the fate of the other prisoners. After several hours, Dimas arrived. He only wanted to speak with the woman and took her along. After an hour both of them returned. I don't know what they talked about, but the woman seemed very confused. She didn't want to tell me anything. Besides Dimas, a few other men were standing around. In the kitchen I asked her what was going on. She told me that Dimas wanted to take her along, and she wasn't supposed to tell me about it. "You have to decide that," I told her. "But I don't want to go along, I want to stay here," she said, and began to cry. I couldn't take it anymore and went to Dimas. "Why do you want to take the woman along?" I asked. "Why did you tell her not to say anything about it to me?" I also put it to him that he had the authority to do what he wanted, so I couldn't understand why everything here was happening so secretively and personally, without commands. If she would go along with him, Dimas wanted to set her free near Waslala. I suggested that he let them all go free. I told the people that they could go, that they were free. But when Dimas saw that the woman was leaving too, he went wild and released the safety on his carbine. I became very uneasy—it looked like I should release the safety on mine, too. Of course he hadn't told me what he had planned for the woman, but it was clear to me what was going on. The two left. What happened to them afterward, I don't know.

Plan C was called off in June. Military action against Matagalpa was supposed to be an essential factor, but the fighting units did not achieve their goal.

After this incident, I moved my troops to the Matagalpa region. I had 30 people with me and then Jonathan, from the "Jorge Salazar" unit, joined us. He also had 30 people so we again became a group of 60. Near Guanaguazo we immediately engaged a militia unit. The new group didn't have enough fighting experience, in my opinion. They fired all-out in all directions until I ordered them to cease fire. It was totally crazy. We had just entered our battle zone and in this first encounter, that lasted about 30 minutes, they had already used up almost our whole supply of ammunition. The militia followed us to another encounter near Tagua. This battle lasted two hours. Our unit had the first two deaths.

We then moved on to the Yunani area, where we had our last battle. The march was long and some of our people simply deserted along the way. We were followed constantly, and in the end we hardly had any ammunition. That's why we had to keep marching, because we could no longer win a battle. As the group noticed what was happening, more and more deserted. Our situation became hopeless. There was no discipline. It was nothing like a real army. I had no desire to fight like this. You quickly become a common criminal. I had, however, taken on a certain task, a certain duty. I had given up my children, my wife, and my work in order to fight. I had no interest in becoming a criminal. That's why I decided to disarm the people.

Jonathan and I analyzed the situation. We had to reach a decision. For Jonathan, the decision was much more difficult. He had fought before in the Sandinista Army, which gave him two problems. He had deserted the Sandinistas and now the FDN too. But we had had it.

I told my people that we had no chance of getting out of this alive. They should go home until we received reinforcements. Then I would call them again. Those who wanted to surrender their weapons to me could do so. I would pitch a camp. To take weapons away from someone in such a situation is suicide. It may be hard to understand but in warfare, where a battle can start any second, it is impossible for a commanding officer to force someone to surrender his weapons. No one likes to be disarmed in such a situation. Nevertheless, many men gave me their weapons and promised to wait for us until reinforcements came. I hid the weapons in the mountains. We dug a ditch, wrapped everything in canvas, covered the weapons with dirt, and marked the spot. Then we got civilian clothing so we could leave the region safely. Of course, we also thought about surrendering, but we were too afraid. We thought it was better to hide in an area where no one knew us.

We then reached Matagalpa, and I found a contact person to get us shoes and clothing. Then I left for Nueva Guinea in the south; the others stayed in Matagalpa. In the village of Nueva Guinea, I looked for a place to stay because I wanted to bring my wife and children there. In the bus on the way back to Matagalpa, a government security agent arrested me.

Isn't it possible that in fact you were ordered by the FDN to set up a new unit in Nueva Guinea?

Who, you mean me?

Yes, of course.

No, if I had wanted that, I certainly would not have deserted. There were other possibilities of organizing a unit.

But that was not desertion. You told the group that they should wait until reinforcements came.

You must understand that in any case I had to find a way out, to keep my own situation from getting any worse. If I had simply told them that I wanted to desert, they would have killed me immediately. That's why I had to find a clever way out.

"'Black Mamba' and 'White Lion' Didn't Make Any Contra Out of Me"
Conversation with Orlando Wayland

What region are you from?

I am a Miskito and I was born in Río Coco on January 7, 1959. I was able to go to school and later became a teacher. It was fun to teach. So I also worked in adult education.

Can you tell us what happened in Francia Sirpi?

It was on December 23, 1983, when suddenly a white jeep drove into the town with our Bishop Schlaefer and the Deacon, Isidoro A. Warado, and Francisco Beker. Father Wendolin Schlaefer was also there. I could see them all, because I still lived in Waspan. Waspan is right on the river, here on our side.

It was about 10 a.m. when they arrived, and, oh, about 4 p.m. they got together with the leaders of our village community. At 6 p.m. they left again. I know so exactly because I had a Seiko watch.

They didn't celebrate any Mass that day. Instead they just gathered with our leaders in the church and conferred. Such a meeting is only for the leaders; we are excluded. When they left again, it was almost dark, the bats were flying around already. I went home and went to sleep.

At 8:00 that night I was startled awake by shots. They were very near. The contras were there and had surrounded the whole town. They shot with everything they had. My heart beat very wildly. I was pretty excited and got up and looked out of the hut. The night was bright. Balls of fire fell from the heavens. They shot fire balls in order to frighten us with them. They wanted to lure people out of their huts.

The contras came into the town. They went into each house and hauled the people out, don't ask me how. With kicks and rifle stocks, the people were torn out of their houses. At the exit from the town, where the road goes towards Santa Clara, we were herded together.

We had to take with us what we could carry of our things, right away. About 1,200 Miskitos live in our town and it was almost 2 a.m. before everyone was brought together. They bound me with a rope since I work for the government as a teacher. Everyone who is paid by the government was tied up, the social workers and the teachers.

Did you know some of the contras?

Yes, I knew many of them. The one from MISURA who led them had been in school with me.

Were there also relatives of the village people among them?

No, they were from another community, they didn't belong to any family in the village.

Was anyone injured in this action?

They murdered two health workers, shot them. One was named Richard, the other. . . .I can't remember right now. They also murdered the brother-in-law of Francis Beker.

You said that you were bound securely?

Yes, tightly and to one another. A guard with an M-60 was supposed to watch over us. The other contras ripped off everything which they could take with them. They completely emptied the store of Jose Zuñiga, and consumed everything edible. Things that last longer they took with them. They did the same thing in the other stores, like that of Otto Borst who also had clothes. They took everything with them, pants, shirts, everything.

The Bishop and the clerics came and took the weakest women

and old people with them in vehicles and traveled to Wiskonsin. It is three hours from Francia Sirpi to Wiskonsin. All the others followed on foot.

How did the leaders of the village community act?

Our leaders are also our clerics. Before, we had a council of elders in our village community—no longer. All of them were surprised, completely surprised. Suddenly, in the middle of the night, the entire village is attacked. Somehow, something didn't figure. In the morning the Bishop arrived unexpectedly, and at night the village community was attacked. I believe that our clerical leaders knew everything, knew exactly what was up and they were amenable to it. Indeed, they took along the weakest women and old people in a car to Wiskonsin. From there you can't go any further by car. The Bishop stopped his jeep there and when we arrived in Wiskonsin, we had to arrange ourselves in marching columns. We didn't stop. The contras said we had to go on immediately.

Didn't the bishop speak to you at all?

With the people certainly, but not with our small group of bound men.

Didn't anyone tell you why all this happened? Didn't they give you a reason?

What should they have said? Get up, we are going to Honduras, to the promised land? Meanwhile, the contras began to get drunk from the stolen bottles and got crazier and crazier, fell down, staggered, lay on the ground or fired their guns in the air. They were drunk out of their minds. The children and women cried. Many were pregnant, the younger ones gripped the old under their arms and helped them. The contras ran around the whole time and fired shots for no reason. You got very deaf from the sound of the shots.

The path became worse and worse. Often mud came up to

our knees. After Wiskonsin, there are only footpaths left. In Francia Sirpi one woman didn't want to come along. She cried and didn't want to go to Honduras. She didn't have a husband but she had to go anyway. Her crying children walked next to her.

Didn't you rest at all?

Not until the next day at 2 p.m. We stopped at one mountain. I was still tied up. They took off our shoes and our shirts; we were allowed to keep only our underpants. They must have thought we would run away. Well, I would have used the first opportunity to do so.

About 500 contras were gathered on this mountain. They had to watch us and make everything secure. The leader was Juan Solórzano—they called him "White Lion." The acting commander was Orlando Martínez, the one who had gone with me to school in Waspan. He was the political leader. His code name was "Machixe," which means "Black Mamba" in our language. Then there was another man named Mitchell. He had also studied with me. He was an officer. It was a mixed unit. Miskitos, Sumus, ex-Guards of Somoza, ex-EEBIs, all mixed up.

The commander ordered them to kill three cows they had taken with them. We were supposed to march for five days beginning the next day, so the commander ordered his men to cook a meal not only for that evening but also for the following day. The women made a fire and began cooking. The contras were drunk again that evening and began to shoot. I think if the army had come, it would have been child's play.

Why didn't the Sandinista army come?

There was no army in that area. Francia Sirpi was far away. At 5 a.m., we broke camp. After five or six hours, the army overtook us anyway. There was a big battle and we had to go faster. Most of the contras stayed behind and fought against the army. We couldn't go forward fast enough so Solórzano ordered us to throw away everything that we had with us.

Were you bombed? The newspapers said that you had been bombed.

No, the one battle was all and we weren't bombed in it. The rest of the march lasted the entire day and night until we came to a bridge. Everything was checked there. I had 200 córdobas with me, my savings. They were taken from me. Everything that the people had on them was now taken away from them. Three women gave birth on the march. As soon as a child was out, the umbilical cord was cut and they had to go on immediately. But all the children survived, I think. The women went through a lot and then had to carry their newborn babies in their arms. "If you stand still, you will surely die," they were told. They went on. They were taken with us into the camp. I don't know what happened to them.

How long was the march to the camp?

Four days and nights we marched. When we finally came to Río Coco, Steadman Fagoth Müller, the chief of the general staff of the MISURA, was already there to receive us. He had on a camouflage suit and military boots, and an American cap on his head. There were four contras around him. I know Fagoth, he is from Esquipulas on the Río Coco. Solórzano handed over the bound men to him. Fagoth asked me why we would work for the Communists. Meanwhile, they also brought the dead and wounded contras from the battle with the army. Fagoth screamed at us: "You will pay for these dead and wounded!" He gestured towards us. We were still tied up. Fagoth called a soldier whom they called "Camare," torture slave. He pushed us to the river and just threw us down the slope. Then they beat each of us, from all sides. I lay with my head in the water and couldn't even cry out.

What happened to the rest of the group?

They were brought across the river in boats. You can't get through at that point on foot, the river is too deep. About 30 people fit into the boat. So it took a very long time until everyone was on the other side. There we were grouped together again. Fagoth commanded all the males over 12 years of age to be singled out. He told us that many fighters had fallen, that they needed new soldiers. There were lots of young men among us. But several men did not want to be separated from their families. They wanted to go with them to the camp. Fagoth agreed to that. Only 42 men wanted to fight with MISURA. They were started marching, and had another hour to go, up to a big road which, I think, led to Mocorón. All the others were brought into the camp of Wampu Sirpi. Our small group had to go two hours further to a sign that said, "Command Post."

What happened at the command post?

Milton Fagoth Müller, the brother of Steadman Fagoth, was waiting for us. His code name is "El Bravo." The contras never use their real names, always their code names. I knew several of the men, knew how they looked, but I didn't know their code names.

The 42 who wanted to fight with the MISURA were trained. They stuck us into a cell. It was actually a cage of bamboo. We couldn't stand upright but could only squat and kneel. There was no roof. We were exposed without protection to the heavy rainfalls. We had to crawl though a hole into the cage and were tied to a stake without pants, shoes, and shirts. We were so exhausted that practically nothing mattered to us. We had to wait forever. Then two of them came and bellowed: "We are supposed to move you to other quarters. Get ready." But nothing happened, we had to wait some more.

The next day, three of them came, among them one woman. Her name is Gretel Domingo. One of the men was Manuel Escobar. He comes from Asang, from the Río Coco. The other was a Sumu from Musabas. The three tortured us for days. They threw us into a giant ant hill—look, you can see the scars that I still have on my body. Or they doused us under water. This was the worst for me. I begged them just to put a bullet through my head rather than push me under water. Each time I became unconscious. They also simply tied us up in the water, from sunset to sunrise. It was muddy, stinking water, and it went up to my nose. At night it was unbelievably cold in the water. For something special, our torturers made us empty the outhouses in the camp with our bare hands.

They did all this to us to find out what we knew about the military actions of the army. We didn't know anything about that. They just believed that if we worked for the government, we would have to know everything about the army. I am a teacher and know everything about education. I have no idea about military actions. But they didn't understand that. In our village community there were no militias, no army.

How long did these interrogations last?

They tortured us for two months. Then there was also political instruction. Each night a priest read the Mass and preached a long time: "You are Miskitos and must support our battle. We must destroy these communists who oppress our tribe. We must bring more Miskitos here, because we need young fighters for our cause."

I also saw Martin Macoy at this command post. He was responsible for the personnel and was captured in March or April 1983 in Sumubila. Now he fights with the contras. I know him. He is a friend of mine. His family is still in Sumubila.

Did Fagoth come to this camp?

Fagoth spoke to us once. He said that the MISURA was in bad financial shape but that it would be completely different in 1984. He also said that Bishop Schlaefer had helped us very much; he had spoken up for his Miskitos.

Do you know when the military leadership of the MISURA was established?

The "Commander in Chief" is Steadman Fagoth Müller. His code name is "Dama." They say "Dama" to him in Miskito. The guards call him "Old One," which is simply the translation of "Dama." Raúl Tobías was there. He comes from Waspan, from Río Coco, Walter Carvajal from Bilwaskarma, Horwarth Carvajal, who is the brother of Walter, Lehart Mora—I think he comes from there too, and Fedingo Martínez, he comes from Asang from Río Coco. A Sumu is also involved, who comes from Ulnas.

You also fought with the contras. How did that happen?

One day the comandante told me that I had the choice of being taken to another camp, but it was a long way and he could guarantee nothing, or I could join the revolutionary forces to free the Miskitos. They sent me then to a training camp. The comandante there was from the Somoza National Guard, from Masaya, "Chang" was his name. There were two trainers. One was called "Mercenario," who came from the Pacific. The other was called "Samba," a sturdy black who was bigger than all of us. He was from Bluefields. The order was clear: whoever fled the camp was shot on the spot. He who deserted can choose: a shot in the head or the back.

I was very sad during this time, my family was far away, my children and I in the camp. Often I didn't sleep a wink at night. We got almost nothing to eat, a flat cake made from corn and beans, morning, noon, and night. There was nothing at all to drink. The commanders, on the other hand, had it really good. They ate meat and everything good. That was a shame. They were well-paid and we received nothing at all, not even a centavo. They had not only money but also women. There were also a few women among the troops. They were trained but not so harshly as the men.

How were you trained?

There were different levels. At first we practiced how to attack a town, a military post, a bridge, how you take a prisoner, or destroy a health station.

Then we were trained with weapons, how to take weapons apart and clean them, and how to use them. First there was the M-17, the 60mm and 80mm mortars, the M-79 grenade-launcher, and the M-60 machine-gun, the FAL, the Chinese AK and simple carbines. Yes, we were trained on those. Then we learned to handle mines: mines which could destroy entire bridges or which were placed under roads. In our group, we had two trainers for 64 soldiers. "Mercenario" taught us how to use the mines. There were also special mines which were used if you wanted to lay a trap for a big patrol, let's say at least 100 men. This mine has a long fuse. You hide in the bushes and when the patrol comes into sight, you light the fuse, very simple. Another mine is the anti-tank mine. It weighs close to 30 pounds and is rolled onto the street. When a vehicle of 600 pounds travels over it, it explodes. Yes, it must be at least 600 pounds, a heavy weight must pass over it or else it doesn't explode. Another mine, as we called it, was simple TNT, with which bridges are bombed. The newest explosive that we received was white phosphorus. You destroy schools or health posts with that. They are left in the wall and after one hour they explode.

How were you furnished with food and clothes?

I remember exactly. I was still in the camp then. Once I saw how an olive-green helicopter from the gringos landed on a small slope at the camp and brought weapons and uniforms. We were dressed entirely in blue—blue pants, blue shirts, tie boots like the Americans, that was our uniform.

On another day, a small two-motor plane arrived. It brought foodstuffs, sacks of beans and rice. I saw the writing on the sacks: they were from Honduras. Once a big olive-green airplane from the gringos came, too. They threw foodstuffs from the air, sacks full of cans. Once the gringos themselves came into the camp.

"Chang" said that they had fought in Vietnam. They just watched over the training. They didn't train themselves but organized everything so that it all went right.

Did they speak Spanish?

They spoke in their language. Fagoth speaks three languages: Spanish, Miskito, and English.

Who received training?

In the camp there were also young fellows, 12 years old. For them the training is murderous. We had to get up at 3 a.m. and sometimes we went to bed not before 6 or 7. Every day was the same, and also the meals. Who can stand that? There was never any meat. Only recently have I had meat to eat. At the beginning there were 64 of these boys. Seven fled immediately, they simply couldn't stand it—the hunger. Sometimes they went into the kitchen just to look, and even for that they were punished severely. Their hair was cut very short, a bald strip around the head, almost like a bishop; it looked almost laughable, but it was a punishment. A man had to control himself, to be a man means to be able to stand anything.

Did you also have code names?

Yes, each received his code name, but not until he was sent out of the camp. We didn't have any yet.

Were you also in other training camps?

No, but we were told of the others. There was a training camp which they called the "Chinese Stronghold." There the trainers were Koreans and Vietnamese. That's what they said, at least. They wore black uniforms, had their hair cut very short, just like Chinese. There the people were specially selected, they had to be fast, fast in their reactions, because they are trained to be special commandos.

Another training camp is called TA. That means Air Troop. The gringos have that one in their hands, they are the boss there.

The men wear camouflage suits, paratrooper boots, also a camouflage cap, everything American. Naturally a selection takes place. At first everyone must go through a general training camp of the National Guardsmen, like where I was. When they notice that you react quickly, then they send you there, you just have to be fast.

In the refugee camps, people are told again and again: if you don't take part in the war, then you can't go back—you have to stay here as a punishment. Thus, most fight simply out of fear, because everyone wants to return to their villages. And what can you do if they say that you can't get over the river any other way?

The clerics play a big role in this too. They have the Bible, they hold masses every day. Most are Moravian pastors, but there are also Catholics.

What was your first action?

One morning after roll-call we were told: "The plan is to bring the people from Sumubila to Honduras." After two weeks training, it went very fast. I sat for two months in a cage, captured. Then they worked on me for two weeks to go over to the contras, and then came two weeks of training. That makes three months in all. Before we set out for Nicaragua, they had already sent 350 men to Salto Grande, 500 to drag the people from Sumubila, and 30 to capture Canas, a strong point here in the area. Everything was supposed to happen more or less simultaneously. Canas was supposed to be attacked to lure the Sandinista army into a trap.

Six men remained in La Esperanza to receive the people from Sumubila. We formed one troop of six, selected from 42, and were assigned to besiege Wiskonsin. As I said, Wiskonsin is very near Francia Sirpi. "Chang" took command; the second in charge was a Miskito named Pasmaya; the third was Carlos, an ex-National Guardsman; the fourth was a Honduran National Guardsman whom we called Teson. He was a member of the so-called "special commando for night actions." A woman also came with us, who was a nurse, to give first aid. The sixth was a radio operator. He made radio contact between the separate units.

We left on March 19—the others had already set out toward Sumubila, Salto Grande, La Tronquera, and La Esperanza. The first night we spent right on the bank of the Río Coco, near a house belonging to the Porras family, who help the contras get the people across the river.

Our leaders explained to us that we were marching to Wiskonsin to set a trap for the army while the others brought the people from Sumubila.

I had been assigned a 60-mm machine gun and in addition 1,000 rounds of ammunition. My assistant had an AK-Chino. Each battery of ammunition weighs five pounds. I had four, which was terribly heavy. I had received only one pound of salt for food, exactly one pound. According to the command, we were supposed to sustain ourselves from leaves and to steal livestock where we could: chickens, pigs, cows. We were supposed to salt the meat and eat it. Outside of that, I received a few pills to quiet my hunger. The pills don't let you feel the hunger so much. In reality we couldn't steal any livestock anywhere, and had to live on leaves. Once we also found a kind of banana that you can cook, which we wolfed down, green as it was. And once we found yucca root.

By March 20, we had already crossed the Río Coco. I didn't allow myself to think about what lay before me. If the army really crossed our path, I was done for. By then, I was already a person who no longer existed. My only thought was to flee as soon as an opportunity presented itself. But I didn't know the way very well. We walked eight days. At night one group stood guard, the other slept. We slept on the ground, wrapped in blankets.

Naturally there were animals in this area, but we didn't find any to eat. Snakes and also small tigers live in this area, but we never saw any. We had weapons—perhaps they were frightened of us.

When we came near Wiskonsin, we were in 3 groups of 12

people each, with 6 leaders. That made 42 of us. Our leader was called Streuhundert, Lieutenant Streuhundert, also a Miskito. We were a mixed group, Miskitos, Sumus, National Guardsmen. The leaders look at you from top to bottom and too bad if you try to flee; then you are shot immediately.

Did you meet the Sandinistas?

Towards mid-day we arrived near Wiskonsin. I was just looking for the first best opportunity to flee. I had the idea of spilling the water out of my canteen and asking permission to go get water. I took only the AK-Chino with me and the canteen. I knew a little path which led from the river directly to La Tronquera. But that path didn't exist anymore, there was nothing but the thickest bushes everywhere. So I filled my canteen and turned back again.

Weren't you afraid of surrendering yourself to a Sandinista unit?

I knew how to do it. You hold your weapon over your head and surrender.

When did you flee?

Soon it began to rain, through the entire night. I didn't shut an eye. The next day I saw the orange tree. It hung full of ripe oranges. I asked permission to go get a few oranges. My boss gave me permission. We were all very sick from hunger. I ran away and also found, luckily, the path which led to the main road. I had only a blanket, an American blanket which they had given to us to protect us from the cold. I ran and didn't stop running until I came to Francia Sirpi. It was already late and the sun went down. To calm my hunger, I picked four chestnuts.

Did you meet people in Francia Sirpi?

No one. No one is there any more. They took them all, you know, to Honduras. The village is a sad sight, the houses are empty, the pigs and cows are dying, everything is awful. And the people up there in the camps...

On the way to La Tronquera there is a bridge. I spent the night near there, got up very early and walked further, I ate nothing the entire day, hunger tortured me, but I had to go on. Near La Tronquera there is a bridge called Liquus, which is guarded by the army, that I knew. There I turned myself in. First the soldiers questioned me, then they brought me two plates of food, real food with rice and beans and meat. That was a joy.

Then I was brought to my family who live here in Puerto Cabezas. I also have family in Managua, and others in Sumubila. But right now, I am staying for a while in Puerto Cabezas and I want to work again as a teacher.

"You Can Only Build the Internal Front Like a Fish in Water"

Conversation with Pedro Espinoza Sánchez

I am an agricultural technician. I studied at the International Agricultural School in Rivas, in southern Nicaragua. Right after the triumph of the revolution, I began working at the Julio Buitrago Sugar Mill [named for a Sandinista hero].

How did you establish contact with the opposition?

The first contacts were made in August or September, 1981. Clemen Araica, who now lives in Honduras, spoke to me. Earlier her husband had been a colonel in the National Guard. She asked me if I wanted to work with the "Legion of September 15." Back then it was in its infancy. The most important task was building units and recruiting new people. That can only be done by someone who has a big circle of friends, and I had one. I had many friends. I played baseball, attended church regularly and even played in some bands because it was fun to make music. Besides, I also worked in the Julio Buitrago Sugar Mill. There I was a foreman of the fieldworkers, and I had about 1,000 workers under me. Naturally I had to be very careful, since it was very risky to drop even one word about the counterrevolution. Cleverly, and using intuition, I was finally able to filter out of the mass of workers several people who seemed "vulnerable." Almost all of them came from families of the National Guard. Several also had relatives in the clink. Later I joined the group that Clemen Araica had organized at the "Industrial Química de Nicaragua" distillery.

I was known there as a music teacher, but my real duty was to spread political information. My contact was a man who lived with a priest.

My assignment was to recruit people. We established a file for every person we recruited. This included all personal information. At the end came the oath. The most important slogans then were: "With God and patriotism, we will defeat Communism," and "Nicaragua will again be a republic." That's what we operated with. In the oath, each person swore that he would fight to the death against the Revolution. After writing out this oath, he became a member of the organization. When I really think about it, we had no special ideology of our own. The basic idea was that we were living in a time of war, and that we needed to use the means of war to force the present government to its knees. Afterwards we would be able to elect a liberal/conservative government in Nicaragua. It wasn't hard to explain to people that things were not running smoothly with the Sandinistas in power. That was already clear to the people working with us. I think it took about four months for the Legion to disband and break off all contact with Honduras. I still continued to meet with Clemen.

In early 1982, I quit the job at the sugar mill. It was actually more of a personal problem, because I argued with a policeman whom I had known before. He now wore the uniform and had become someone, and wanted to settle an old account from school days. No one expected me to still be carrying my old weapon. As I defended myself and shot the policeman, the others overcame me and threw me in jail. That ended my job at the sugar mill and I went to Matagalpa. There I knew the previous director of the Department of Agriculture (under Somoza) fairly well, and he promised to get me a job on a coffee hacienda. However, I was able to stay at his hacienda as his assistant. On Christmas Eve 1982, as we celebrated the holiday with family and friends, he spoke openly about the FDN for the first time. At first I didn't want to join, thinking that he was only provoking me, but he wouldn't let up. During the following days he continued to bring up the subject and asked my opinion. He wanted to invite me to a meeting of the FDN unit in Matagalpa. It consisted of a lawyer, a construction engineer, a master mechanic and a plantation owner. Slowly I began to appreciate their view of things and became a member of their unit. Here again it was my task to recruit new people.

At this time, four or five armed groups were operating in the heart of the Matagalpa mountains. We had nothing to do with them. Each had about 30 to 40 people and all were ex-National Guardsmen, common criminals or militiamen who had changed sides. They had absolutely no political line. They were real gangs, who made the area dangerous. All of them operated on their own. I became well acquainted with one of the gang leaders. His name was "Calimán." Because we also needed armed men, we thought about going back to these groups to win them over to the ideas of the FDN. We had to see how we could undertake armed struggle in the central parts of the country. The social status of the important members of our unit, like the lawyer or the engineer, practically prohibited establishing contact with the people in the mountains. Were they supposed to get on a horse and ride through the jungle in order to talk to the gang leaders? My God, that was impossible. It was clear that only I could make that contact. They didn't need to explain more. I understood immediately.

I did, however, make my situation clear to them. I told them that I had a family to feed. Until then I was receiving my wages on the hacienda, and I was able to make ends meet. I therefore requested a certain percentage of my wages as pay and a few other guarantees—for instance, the chance to leave the country if something went wrong. Anybody who gets into such a situation must keep a clear head and make a good deal. I didn't want to stay a little nobody who does the work for others. I wanted access to certain information and decisions. I simply wanted to have the freedom to work as I saw fit. I even asked that all my conditions be written down and that the political leaders of the FDN sign them. At this time José Fernando Cardenal was in charge. They immediately agreed. The pay I received was about twice as much as I had earned before. The hacienda paid me 4,500 córdobas, and they offered me 10,000 córdobas. I'm not trying to say that I took the job just to earn a lot of money, but it wasn't bad.

I had signed up and immediately began preparations. I had to find the gang leaders. That alone was a great risk, since I had to slip through all the Sandinistas' cordons. To avoid being caught immediately, I had to think through very carefully how to reach my goal and the best ways to conceal this goal. First I had to find the right men. This process made me very familiar with the region around Matagalpa. The people here who oppose the Sandinistas are mainly rich farmers. On the one hand, they can't read or write, but on the other hand they have 500 to 600 cattle and sometimes over 200 hectares of land. They are real farmers and don't know beans about politics or history. They have also never been hungry. These were the people that we had to win over.

The farmers, who were almost little plantation owners, employed 80 to 90 shepherds and farmhands who were totally dependent on them. What the farmer said, went. I had to begin with the farmers. The people in our unit gave me total logistical support. They liked the way I attacked things. First I got false papers in order to move freely. Then I needed weapons, so I orchestrated my own ambush: a landowner from San Ramón agreed that we could "steal" the old weapons he had from before (a few M-16 rifles and some flints) and make it look like an assault. It went smoothly. Now at least we had some weapons. After this successful operation, I asked to be made military leader of the FDN unit in Matagalpa. This move put me on the same level as the political leader of the unit.

As a second step, I wondered how I could establish contact with "Calimán" and "El Justiciero," the gang leaders. We knew that they operated in a radius of 80 kilometers around Río Blanco and that the contact person was a Peruvian landowner named Tobías Hernández. He had a cattle ranch in the area. He let the people pitch camp on his land, provided them with cattle, gave them money and also supplied them with medicines. He had even recruited people for these gangs, people from the Matiguás area. It was through him that I made contact with the gangs. I was considered an expert on cattle-raising and was to go look at the Peruvian's cattle. I did not attract any attention. It seems really crazy— there were times when Sandinista soldiers gave me a lift in their vehicles when I was hitchhiking. They would stop, and I sat between the soldiers.

The Peruvian was an educated but also very cautious man. I think he was a father-figure to the men. They all blindly obeyed him. He told the gang members that I was from the FDN and wanted to give them a few suggestions. After several days of negotiations, I was allowed to visit their camp. That was in September, 1982. "Calimán" and "El Justiciero" fought for the same cause, but each led his own group. We met at a remote spot. Both gang leaders had their bodyguards along. I was alone and only carried my revolver. I first told them what the FDN wanted, and what its political goals were. They completely agreed with us that we must fight against communism by all available means. I told them that we could supply them with weapons and ammunition if they joined us, and that we were not fighting alone, but that we could count on the complete support of the gringos. I made it clear that we had everything—money and weapons—and that we could begin our common struggle against the Sandinistas tomorrow. They would become part of a larger army, and would no longer move through the mountains in this miserable way, robbing farmers. They only had 20-caliber flints and perhaps several hundred rounds of ammunition. It must have had an effect on their fighting spirit to have little more than a few hunting rifles against a well-equipped army with automatic weapons. It was therefore relatively easy to convince them that it would be in their best interests to join the FDN, and that that was the only way they could survive.

"Calimán" is a farmer and comes from Río Blanco. He is illiterate. His real name is Pedro Cardoza; "Calimán" is his code name. He's already had a wild past. After the victory of the revolution he joined the militia and was soon sent to a training program in Jalapa. There he learned a bit about war tactics. The Sandinistas trusted him and put him in command of 12 men in the militia. He lost little time and took off for the mountains with them. They and their weapons were the basis of his gang.

The other, "El Justiciero," whose real name is Eduardo Colera, comes from Boaco. He even owned a small farm, but was tired of working the land and took his people to the mountains.

These were the people whom I had to win over to our goals because they knew the area well and were experienced soldiers. I put all my chips on one card and made it clear that I was now the military leader of the area and that they would be subject to my commands if they wanted to work with us. I could hardly believe it, but they agreed without batting an eyelash and asked for no noteworthy conditions.

In September, 1982, those Sandinista bloodhounds found out where we were operating and sent a patrol out for us. We did have really good people, but were still not in a position to try a skirmish with the Sandinistas. It would have been crazy. There were 40 of us and about 600 from the Sandinista army. We had the short end of the stick. We had no choice but to retreat farther back into the mountains. It was a damned difficult time; we hardly had any food. I can remember weeks when we ate nothing for four or five days. Some got fed up, put their rifles against a tree and left. They simply deserted. This was terrible for our morale. One day I couldn't stand it any more and I called them all together and told them that they could all go home. I explained that I would call them back when I saw a new possibility. I took care of the weapons, wrapped them up well and stored them in a secure hiding place. Three men stayed with me.

We had to walk three days to escape the Sandinista encirclement. We came to a hacienda where I simply stole a vehicle and drove to Boaco. In Boaco I took a bus to Managua. Naturally I immediately tried to contact my people in Matagalpa, but no one was there anymore. When they found out that the Sandinista army was chasing us, they simply packed their bags and left for Honduras. Only one of them, the lawyer, went to Costa Rica. When I heard that, I also decided to head for Costa Rica. I rode to Rivas and from Rivas to Peñas Blancas, the border town. But I had no papers. I exchanged a few córdobas for colones and went along the border until I came to a cow pasture where I crossed. If you know the area well, then the border is easy to cross. The cows were standing around the pasture. I began to drive them as if I were the cattle herder, and as I got very close to the border I simply jumped over the barbed wire. About five in the afternoon I arrived in La Cruz, a town pretty far into Costa Rica. By nightfall I was unable to continue; it was better to sleep there until the next morning. In the morning I took a bus to San José. Even in San José, it was extremely difficult to find quarters without papers. That afternoon I accidentally met two Nicaraguans who had a small hotel in San José; I could stay with them. Then I had an idea and went to a private radio station called Radio Reloj, the next day. I gave them a type of search announcement: So-and-So is here in San José and wants to meet Mr. So-and-So. In less then 24 hours, the people I was looking for reported to me.

Soon I was able to make a call to Chicano Cardenal in Los Angeles. He promised to come to San José as soon as possible, to discuss further plans with me. But it was almost Christmas and he couldn't get a flight. He arrived in early January. During our first phone conversation, he had already told me that he wanted to separate from the FDN and work further on his own plans. I soon saw that he didn't want to work with the FDN, but he did copy its structure. When he arrived, we discussed our plans for the future. His plan was actually the birth of the FRIN (Nicaraguan Internal Front). The leaders were Chicano Cardenal and Mariano Mendoza. They wanted me to stay in Costa Rica and coordinate things from there, but they hadn't reckoned on how I felt. I wanted to be in on the action in Nicaragua. It was clear to me that the [Sandinista] system could be endangered only by establishing an effective Internal Front. I stayed in Costa Rica 17 days. We worked out a plan of action which Chicano and I signed. Alejandro Martínez was named military director of the General Staff. He was a Cuban with much experience in guerrilla warfare and also a paid advisor to the Costa Rican Secret Service. Chicano went back to the U.S., and I returned to Nicaragua by the same route. This time I was supplied with enough dollars for my assignment in Nicaragua.

It was clear to me that we could not begin military action yet. We had to concentrate completely on building our network of units. That's why we agreed in San José to send 40 people each to Costa Rica. Martínez offered to train the people in guerrilla tactics along with the Costa Rican guards. This training was under the direction of the Israelis at that time. Mendoza had also given me a number of other contacts who were able to offer me good logistical support. They were members of the Christian Union, CTN, and Catholics who knew me from before. However, I had no idea that they were with the contras. From these circles I had to find suitable people to send to Costa Rica for training. To do this, I contacted Dr. Miriam Argüello and a certain Carlos of the CTN.

It was important to me to be my own boss. I had control over the money and decided what it should be spent on. I now had the rank of General Staff leader for the Internal Front.

When did you take the code name "El Pez," the Fish?

I always signed my orders P.E.S., that is, Pedro Espinoza Sánchez, my real name. It soon became common for people to call me PES. I think many people did not know that *pez* (fish) is written with a 'z'. I also think that people called me fish because I was so hard to catch. "El Pez" was not my only code name; some knew me as "Napoleón," others as "José Moreno," and others as "Halcón," (Falcon). My driver's license, which I got in Matagalpa, was issued to the name Hernán. That's why some people called me Hernán.

Things were running fairly well then—the building of the units and all the other things, too. Suddenly, in March of 1983, the aid stopped. Things became clear when I received news from Chicano, who told me that there was no more money for the Internal Front. He didn't want to lie to me; they simply took away his support. Those were the hard facts. He would continue in solidarity with our struggle, but we had to do what we could without money from him. The result was that I could not send any more people to Costa Rica for training. So far we had sent only two groups of ten people each. I cut off all contact and explained to the people in the cells that we would have to go into a holding pattern.

Then the same thing happened as before. Contact people from the FDN spoke to me. They knew everything about how I had set up secret cells. In early April, a courier brought me a letter. His code name was "Maruca." I was dumbfounded, but the letter was signed by the General Staff of the FDN. It was from Calixto Ordúñez himself. I was to go to Honduras as fast as possible; the FDN General Staff people wanted to have an in-depth talk with me.

I set off right away by car to Ocotal, and from there on foot across the border to Honduras. That took almost 18 hours. Once you cross the high mountains of Dipilto, you are already over the border. My contact was an officer in the Honduran army. He put a car and a couple of bodyguards at my disposal. We drove to the Las Manos base. There I was introduced to Lieutenant Santos Rivera, who was in command of the border area called "El Paraíso." He had me brought to Danli. After a day at the best hotel in Danli, an officer from the FDN came to pick me up. He was in civilian clothing but armed, of course. I was amazed at how well the FDN was supported in Honduras. They could do practically anything they wanted. They not only informed the Secret Service of Honduras, DIN, about their activities; the two FDN officers even had officers' identification from the Honduran Secret Service. Soon Dr. Indalecio Alaniz, "El Tulián," of the FDN political leadership arrived. We drove with him to Tegucigalpa. There I personally got to know Emilio Echaverry, ex-major of the National Guard and head of the FDN. We conversed for almost three days in the hotel. I had to maintain my position. That was the most important thing to me; I could not be subordinate to anyone. Never in my life was I a soldier, and I am not used to saying: "At your command, sir." No, that is not my style. From the start I made this clear to "Fierro." He had no problems with that, and immediately began calling me by my first name.

"You are here in Honduras, I am in Nicaragua. You have the logistics, the weapons, I have the people." That was the starting point which I made clear to them. I told them of my connection to Chicano and that naturally I was ready to work with them. After our conversations, we really didn't have any differences of opinion anymore. They assured me that they would support me, but only under the condition that my people would no longer be trained in Costa Rica, but rather in Honduras. We also agreed that they would show me various routes for crossing the border unmolested. They again stressed how important it was to have close relations and cooperate with the Catholic Church. They gave me 300,000 córdobas. That was not very much. But they promised to send me weapons, grenades and plastic explosives. I now had practically everything that I would need for building the units. It was important that the supply routes worked. We now had a car and we took people to Ocotal, where we were told which route was secure for crossing. For the trip back, I tried one of the routes and put a small stash of weapons in a secure place. In Ocotal a jeep was waiting, just as we had agreed. Our communications were carried over the September 15th Radio Station. We had agreed on a certain code for our radio messages.

Practically nothing had changed in my working methods. The only difference was that I was now sending people to Honduras. The people we sent were mainly skilled workers; they had received some training. There were even some academics. Almost all of them were in the CTN union. We even sent a news broadcaster to Honduras for training—Alejandro Acevedo from Radio Corporación. However, he stayed there and now works for the FDN station, Radio 15. He has even become their director. We sent women teachers and female students—everyone capable of learning how to use weapons and explosives. They learned how to use C4, C3, TNT and grenades, and received guerrilla training. At this time the FDN was channelling the first fighting troops into Nicaragua. Our plan was to supplement the armed struggles in northern Nicaragua with sabotage and terror performed by our Internal Front.

We prepared explosives to destroy bridges and factories. The training was focussed on this goal. I was certain about the military importance that these actions could have. It's a different story when the international press reports on battles in the mountains 200 kilometers from Managua, than when they report an explosion at a factory or a business in the capital city. Our job was armed resistance from the inside outwards. To do it, we needed people who were able to carry out this type of attack. Until now we had concentrated on the cities, but we now wanted to extend our activities to the rural areas. Our idea was to get people who wanted to fight against the regime and organize them properly.

At this time the FDN had three governing bodies: the Strategic Command, the General Staff and the political leadership. The Strategic Command planned the actions of the whole organization on a national level. The General Staff was assigned to carry out those plans. The political leadership provided the orientation that corresponded to the plans. I was connected to the strategic command because it was my job to direct the whole operation. My immediate contact man was Commander Echaverry. Another contact was Jacobo, the middle-man between the Argentinian and American advisors. The Argentinian advisor was Colonel Villegas, a stocky character, who was very hot headed. The American's name was Simpson. For them I was the source of news about the situation in the country. In the strategic command we considered what the opportune points in time were for certain large-scale acts of sabotage, like the mining of the harbors or the destruction of the fuel depots from the sea. We decided to train a group of ten men especially for this purpose. These were the best men of the COEP, the Comandos de Operaciones Especiales. They would be trained in Honduras as explosive specialists, and then they could go out individually to certain regions of the country and recruit and train new people. I received the directive straight from the General Staff. I was also called in when new plans were discussed. We prepared everything for the big uprising.

The Internal Front created the necessary conditions with explosions and acts of sabotage that undermined the country's economy. But we had to proceed step-by-step. I always said this to the FDN leaders. I am not the type to exaggerate certain situations or to overestimate fighting capacity. One must always remain realistic. That's why I opposed the sudden idea of making me carry out large bombings. I was supposed to blow up the television transmittor of the most important television station in Nicaragua. I told them they were crazy, absolutely crazy. I asked them if they thought you just go to Channel 6 and then blow it up. Just go to Las Nubes, near Managua, and blow up the station. I worked on a detailed plan which showed them how complicated the connections were, and everything that had to be prepared in order to carry out this action successfully. I noticed that certain plans and commands brought out contradictions between us. They talked day and night about an uprising which would be accompanied by a direct military invasion.

The gringos had brought Marines to Honduras without causing much disturbance, in order to strengthen and organize the FDN's military structure. In Tegucigalpa, people said that 5,000 to 7,000 Marines would provide direct military assistance in an uprising. It was also rumored that the necessary air transport was already on standby. I totally supported this plan strategically. On X day, we of the Internal Front could move into action and operate in coordination with the other military units. But I would like to stress the word (coordination). I insist on this formula because I will have nothing to do with the combat troops of the FDN. My units were autonomous. We were once trapped in a battle which FDN troops had provoked. Since then I have insisted on a strict separation. I sent my assistant to the combat division, and although he told them that he was working with me, he was accused of being a spy and shot. How could I work with such people? No, the Internal Front must be an independent and separate organization. However, before we could carry out our own activities, we had to work on a logistical infrastructure. I observed that the easiest social sector from which to recruit people is the church.

The FDN people were not at all aware that, along with terrorist acts and armed struggle, it is equally important to establish a political basis for this struggle. What good is someone who blows up a station and isn't clear about his political motives? An underground without a set of political ideas is totally impossible or else quickly crumbles. You have to consider whom you are speaking to and whom you can motivate for our work. It is naturally very effective to win over a priest to our cause. He can reach a large circle of people whom he knows, and communicate our political ideas to them. And these are not only the people who go to church every Sunday. There are lay courses, catechism courses, choir groups, all of which can be easily won over when the priest is in our corner. I know several priests from before, but we must try to win over the church hierarchy. It is common for a parish to call two days of spiritual services, and no one finds it unusual when a large crowd of people attends. If 10 or 20 people could perform persuasively at such a weekend, then it might be possible that half of those people would be willing to fight with us. The church is actually an ideal place for something like this. As the Apostle Peter said, ''the Church is the refuge from which you set out to conquer the world.''

It is a great risk to set up a munitions storage area with explosives and other necessary supplies in a private home. To do so in a parish building is not very dangerous. They are always receiving crates and cases of medicines and other aid from the whole world. Nobody counts them; nobody opens them to see what they contain. For example, we packed hundreds of grenades in powdered milk containers. They were never detected. Naturally, the pastor of the parish must agree to this.

The unions are very important too. I belonged to a union and knew how to approach the members. They noticed right away that I was one of them. I quickly established good contacts.

Which organizational stage had you reached by spring, 1984?

Back in November, 1983, when I was developing my strategy, the FDN in Honduras told me that fighter planes were ready to fly. I also toured the military bases at Aguacate, La Fortuna, La Lodosa and Banco Grande in Honduras. The FDN had established regular training schools at some of them. We could therefore expect that soon, at X time, well-trained people would be at our disposal in order to lend military support to a revolt in Nicaragua at strategically important points. I was also told that some governments were merely waiting for the right time to help us. But, as I mentioned, the contradictions and problems were mounting in the FDN. The FDN appointed new leadership for Nicaragua. I was given two additional officers of the same rank. One was to act as coordinator—as a direct connection to the strategic command in Tegucigalpa. His name was Carlos Acevedo; he was a pharmaceutical salesman. He bought medications for Nicaragua and had a special permit for unrestricted travel in and out of the country. The other was the leader of the crafts union in Masaya. That gave him many connections, and he was therefore put in organizational leadership.

[In Nicaragua] I always received the people who were already working for the organization. I informed them about the military plans and our strategic position. After all, I was the military leader of the Internal Front, who controlled arms distribution and gave orders. The people usually said OK and went to work. I seldom concerned myself with ideological issues. The explanation of why the Sandinistas are Communists was the task of the strategic command. I once read *Capital*, by Karl Marx, and a few other books, but that was it. Of course I know a bit about Europe's industrial revolution, about political economy, but it was not my task to specifically point out which political line was good or bad, and it didn't interest me very much.

The differences of opinion between the gringos and the FDN became clear when they killed "El Fierro." I think it happened because he didn't always comply with the directives of the gringos. He isn't the only one who has been pushed out of the way. G-2, whose name was Edgar Hernández and who was an ex-captain in the National Guard, was also liquidated. These two were executed because they didn't blindly follow all the orders they received from the strategic command. The affair was quickly covered up and the word was spread that they had been eliminated because they had embezzled money. This naturally hit me hard because I was the most important man in Nicaragua for "Fierro." His replacement, Enrique Bermúdez Varela, better known under the code name 3-80, didn't even know me. I had never seen him. On the other hand, Carlos Azevedo, who had just been appointed coordinator, had his complete confidence. A cousin or maybe even brother of Azevedo was the famous Comandante Aureliano. Aureliano came to Nicaragua while studying medicine in Mexico. He established units led by Carlos Azevedo. Azevedo always concerned himself more with internal affairs, I assume by order of 3-80. He recruited a certain Raoul to follow me. But I noticed it very fast. So I put a young woman on him, and she gradually pulled all the important details out of him.

These internal conflicts of our triumvirate gradually became unbearable. I invited them all to a meeting at a hacienda near Masaya. It was the "La Francia" hacienda, where we train our explosive experts in theory. At this meeting our tempers became so hot that we suddenly all pulled our pistols. I still don't know why we didn't shoot. But in the end we did make up again. Only later did I notice that all the insults we were flinging had been recorded. The cassette was sent to Honduras. As soon as I heard that, I left for Honduras to explain the situation. I had a passport using the name Carlos Alberto Rogama, a farmer who was long dead. If necessary I could go into hiding. At the airport in Tegucigalpa I first saw what was really happening. I was immediately handed over to the Secret Service, DIN. They drove me to a small FDN house near the airport and began the interrogation. They accused me of not spending the money according to the orders given me. The other arguments ran along the same line as those which bagged "El Fierro." But they wanted to know which units I had established in Nicaragua. I was told to write out the whole network. I refused to talk about it, even though they took me to task. I explained to them that after four years of struggle in Nicaragua, I had enough authority to continue my own strategy. But I could only do that as a free man. I had been captive for 5 weeks, one of them without food nor water. But that did not soften me. After those 5 weeks, I was more resolute than before. Everything indicated they would kill me. That didn't matter to me. There was no way that I would betray the network that I had established.

They took away my rank as comandante and ordered me to care for the wounded in their military hospital. Naturally I protested, but what can you do as a prisoner? The hospital was in a large house about eight kilometers from Tegucigalpa. Military guards made sure that no one ran away. As soon as the wounded can walk again they are sent back to battle. They took everything away from me; I didn't have a penny. Running away was no longer possible. I couldn't find out who planned all of this or why. The General Staff had ordered that I should be treated this way. Since I had been in the confidence of "El Fierro," I also had to be eliminated.

I already mentioned that I was recruited by Clemen Araica. She now had direct access to the General Staff of the FDN in Honduras. When she found out that I was imprisoned, and what was happening to me, she tried to help. One day she came to the hospital where I worked and brought money. She also brought shoes, socks, pants, and a shirt, because all I had was a hospital jacket. She told me to persevere; she would try to get me out. Naturally I didn't tell her that I couldn't take it any longer and was only waiting for an opportunity to escape. It was perfectly clear to me that the FDN leadership would shoot me in an escape attempt. It was easy for them to call me a traitor. Even comandantes like "El Suicida" have been shot. Not only comandantes, but even middle-ranking officers and people with long battle experience have suddenly been shot. Often they were eliminated because of a minor difference of opinion. If they don't want to do it themselves they send you off with an assault detachment of 20 men which is suddenly attacked by a unit of 50 men. The actual reason was always their fear that they would no longer be blindly obeyed. The same with me. It was clear to them that a traitor must be killed, otherwise he would betray the connecting routes and contact people. On the other hand it was impossible not to obey a command in this military hierarchy. If you stand up against it, they put you under military law, call you a deserter and shoot you. That happened to "El Suicida." He didn't follow all of their orders, and they shot him. In those days I also heard that they killed "Abel," from the Secret Service. The fact was that if I were to flee the hospital, I was dead.

I had an idea which they hadn't reckoned with: I simply fled to the Nicaraguan embassy—under a false name, of course. I knew that the Nicaraguan government had passed an amnesty resolution. I still think it was a brilliant inspiration. I introduced myself as Carlos Alberto Rugama. That was the name on my driver's license. I explained that I had made the great mistake of getting involved with the FDN, but they had mistreated me. That's why I wanted to apply in order to go back to Nicaragua. They couldn't find any wrongdoings under the name of Carlos Alberto Rugama, so the embassy decided to grant me asylum.

Today I have to laugh about it. I rode in the car of the Apostolic Nuncio to the Tegucigalpa airport. I left through the diplomatic terminal. I didn't have to wait or show a passport. In the airplane the economic attaché of the Nicaraguan embassy in Tegucigalpa sat next to me. At the airport the Secret Service awaited me. I soon saw that they would ask me only superficial questions, since they had no information under that name [Rugama]. After several interrogations I was set free.

For two weeks I lay low. I used the time to work out a new strategy. I couldn't tell anyone that I was a prisoner of the FDN. That would have aroused suspicion. I had to try to continue working in the Internal Front and show the FDN how much potential I represented. I began by working out a spectacular plan. I contacted old friends like Father Luis Amado Peña, who played a substantial role in coordinating the activities of the Internal Front.

I told him that during my time in Honduras I was assigned to design sabotage plans, which should start with very simple things. Father Peña suggested that we organize a march from one of the large markets of Managua to the central city, where the government palace is. At the same time bombings would be carried out in Masaya and Matagalpa that would greatly affect the country's economy. We wanted to hit the power plant and the telephone office, and also set fire to several busses. June 21, 1984 was the designated day. The struggle had to be continued from the inside; we had to prepare and lead the revolt. I never liked the idea of someone sitting securely outside of the country. The construction of the Internal Front is my business, even though it is naturally much more difficult and more dangerous. But I am a total nationalist and don't want to take orders from outside. I am not the type to take direction from North Americans who expect me to say "at your command." I think that we have no reason to let the Americans continue prescribing to us how we should organize our struggle against the Sandinistas. A person must not lose his grip on reality by following crazy orders that would be pure suicide. One must always try to initiate activities that give you a chance to reach your goal and also stay in one piece.

Several days before June 21, ten Secret Service agents suddenly stood in front of the house in the Bello Horizonte district where I lived. They were heavily armed; I didn't even have a chance to pull my pistol. Well, I could have let them shoot me, but that would have been too cheap.

The position which you described in relationship to the United States reminds me a little of the explanation that Edén Pastora gave for the ARDE.

I do not want to be compared with Edén Pastora. I know him personally and have often spoken with him; and I tell you he has two faces. What he publicly tells the press or radio is pretty far removed from what he really thinks. Edén Pastora receives almost all his weapons from the U.S. I never concerned myself with the U.S. I never went there to beg for money and never went to Costa Rica for money. No, that's not my racket. I always tried to work with Nicaraguans. Sure, it would have been easier to find money and support in other countries. Or simply to stay in other countries and give orders from there, like those in Honduras or Costa Rica. My work was in this country, with the people here, with their daily problems. Only when you are here and live in the same situation as the people, can you lead the struggle from the inside. I am not persuaded by the work of Edén Pastora, that's why you cannot compare me with him.

"I Know What Marxist-Leninist-Stalinists Are Capable Of"

Conversation with Zacarías Hernández

You said that you are a member of the Revolutionary Directorate of the ARDE and General Secretary of "Solidarity of Democratic Nicaraguan Workers." What kind of an organization is that?

It is a union federation made up of four unions: the Alliance of Nicaraguan Workers in Exile, the Union for Education and Learning in Exile, the Union of Harbor Workers in Exile, and the Union of the San Antonio Raw Sugar Factory in Exile.

How many members does it have?

Approximately 2,600 workers living in exile in Costa Rica. But we have many sympathizers in Nicaragua who support our organization.

What does the new situation that has developed as a result of the alliance between the ARDE and the FDN mean for you?

Our organization supports this alliance, which was for all intents and purposes sealed on July 24 with the signing of the document worked out in Panama. This step was necessary in order to finally liberate the Nicaraguan people. We have to gather all our strength to overthrow the Sandinista regime, just as we did in the battle against Somoza. Then we also had to go into exile, seek allies, to overthrow a dictatorship. This one is even worse than the previous one.

Do you really think so?

There are many people who don't want to believe it. But it is true. Somoza represented North American capital, he was a representative of North American capital in Nicaragua. He had to fulfill his mission. It was logical that we were enemies. But today we have been betrayed. Instead of defending the freedom that we won through our victory over the dictator, the country is being handed over to Cuba and Russia.

But there are, however, also four union confederations in Nicaragua. So why do you think it necessary to be pushing yet another union organization in exile?

We were a strong organization in Nicaragua, a strong and independent harbor workers union. It had a strategic meaning. We had a social democratic perspective, represented by the International Transport Worker Society (ITF). I had to leave the country, along with the leaders of the Harbor Workers and Office and Clerical Workers Union of Corinto. Now I have to carry on the battle from here in exile.

The politics of the ARDE consist of armed struggle against the Sandinista government. Is your union participating in it?

That appears logical to us. When there are no other alternatives and all other ways are closed, you have to take up arms. We would like to fight by organizing and doing political work in Nicaragua. But that doesn't work there, the right to strike has been taken away, the....

But in the meantime it has been embodied in law again....

That's correct, but no general amnesty has been proclaimed to let us all return to the country. They are afraid of the real leaders of the workers. When I had to leave I was President of the Union of Harbor Workers and Office and Clerical Workers in the harbor of Corinto. The Sandinistas wanted a Marxist-Leninist social order, built entirely on the Cuban model of Fidel Castro. They talk of Sandinismo but they are Communists. The majority of

Nicaraguans follow the example of Sandino, because he fought for national independence. Most Nicaraguans haven't the vaguest idea about Marxism-Leninism. They simply have nothing in their heads about it, and it is also completely alien to the reality of the Nicaraguan people's lives. The Nicaraguans are a poor people. Nicaragua is no powerful capitalist country, no developed country. Karl Marx developed his social theory in an industrial power, and that was England. That was where the dictatorship of the proletariat was supposed to be erected. But what does that mean in such an underdeveloped country as Nicaragua?

Do you maintain contacts with the unions in Nicaragua or do you work completely independently?

We have no direct organizational connections with any union in Nicaragua. That doesn't mean, however, that we are not in solidarity with all who fight for freedom in Nicaragua. It is the duty of all Nicaraguan workers to fight, in order to shake off the yoke under which they want to harness us. We must lose our fears and unite against the new idiots who have permitted foreigners, Cuban internationalists, to walk through our country armed, for all intents and purposes to occupy our country. And it is not only an affront to us when foreigners in military uniform, with weapons on their shoulders, walk shamelessly through our streets—they also have the say-so in our country and are participating in the repression of our people.

Do you have proof of this? And if it is true, why wouldn't the people rise up against the Sandinistas?

Under Somoza, complete control was exercised over the people and whoever dared to raise his head was beheaded. Today the Sandinista regime exercises a more subtle control, in the name of the people. They have founded neighborhood committees, which control street after street; the strength of the army has increased, and life in Nicaragua is for all intents and purposes completely militarized.

The Nicaraguan Air Force is badly armed, almost non-existent, while the Honduran Air Force has over 80 planes and 5 large airports. And the troops of the FDN and the ARDE comprise 18,000 men. Do you really mean that in this situation the Sandinistas should just stand around with folded arms?

Since the FSLN has been in power, since July 19, 1979, all money has gone into getting armed—even before there was a counterrevolution. Everything points in the direction of having the revolution extended to other countries, with the help of Cuba and the Soviet Union. After Nicaragua should come El Salvador, that was it. Therefore they supported the Salvadoran guerrillas with weapons. And after El Salvador should come Honduras. Then they would be drinking coffee in San José. And the next country would be Chile. Mexico is also on the list, although it doesn't know anything about it at all. One of the comandantes said, word for word, that they don't want to limit themselves to Nicaragua but that the revolution in Nicaragua is just the first step, then all of Central America would follow, including Panama.

I would like to tell you something. I don't know if there is a worse blind man than he who doesn't want to see, or a worse deaf man than he who doesn't want to hear. You just have to approach the situation logically. It's clear that the guerrillas of El Salvador can't get any help from Honduras and just as little from Guatemala. So they get their logistical support from Nicaragua. It can't be any different, either. Why do we need proof, when the realities speak for themselves? The single fact that the General Staff of the FMLN sits in Managua is proof enough.

It would still be interesting, despite all that, to have proof.

Yes, naturally. But you can go further with logic. They smuggle weapons by night, not by day. They have their secret hiding places. On the day when the Salvadoran government shoots down an airplane carrying weapons, that day we will have the proof in our hands.

Let's return once more to the question: What does a union organization have to do with an armed struggle, with sabotage and terror?

In Nicaragua a revolution broke out after the fall of a dictator, and a provisional government was named. Five years have passed and even now no elections are scheduled. The government has not been elected by the people, it is in power though the force of arms. Only when elections have been held, and when they take place legally, can you call those who rise up against the elected government terrorists.

What goes on in the head of a union man when he knows that there is a plan to blow up a cement factory or a refinery or an oil tank, where certainly many people will be blown up too?

I know what the Marxist-Leninist-Stalinists are capable of. Nothing could surprise me. I think the Sandinistas are capable of putting a bomb in the refinery themselves, if they think it's correct—of starting an attack against themselves, in order to lay the blame at the feet of the imperialists.

But we have a concrete case of attacks on the Augusto César Sandino Airport. Half an hour later, around 1,000 people would have been there. Or the planned terrorist acts against representatives of the government, against unarmed people.

Certainly it is always difficult to measure the consequences. But in relationship to the airport, I want to tell you that the aim was to destroy the runway. However, since the airplane was shot at, it collided with the control tower and partially destroyed it.

But civilians lost their lives in this.

That can always happen. We are at war. In the Second World War, lots of innocent people died, more civilians than soldiers. That is unavoidable.

"Somoza Supporters Also Have the Right To Return to Nicaragua"

Conversation with Mauricio Medieta
Member of the Political Directorate of ARDE

In the Costa Rican newspapers, there has been discussion about which of the anti-Sandinista groups is now permitted to call itself the ARDE and who will take over command of the three ARDE camps on the bank of the Río San Juan. Each says, "I'm the one," and contradictions between Edén Pastora and his adviser Carlos Coronel have become public.

It is unfortunately a fact that Comandante Pastora left the ARDE about three months ago. His troops, which were ARDE troops, have advanced far into the interior of Nicaragua. They are already operating in the vicinity of Bluefields, and in the Nueva Guinea area. But units of ours, which are not under the command of Comandante Pastora, are also operating in Nicaragua.

Our military chief is now Comandante Fernando Chamorro, the Supreme Commander. He has his General Staff right inside Nicaragua. And Comandante Pastora has his people with him. We really hope that we will again unify our forces some day because we all pursue a common goal. We respect Comandante Pastora—in any case he is not our enemy. We would not dream of that, and therefore we think that we must overcome the divisions and join together again. Otherwise we are basically just playing into the hands of the FSLN.

But Edén Pastora said in a public debate that you are playing into the hands of the ex-National Guardsmen and the U.S., if you join together with the FDN.

We believe that the members of the FDN are Nicaraguans. To be sure, several were National Guardsmen at the time of Somoza, and others still dream even today, perhaps, of returning to the old times. However, they are in any case in the minority. The large majority, who carry on the battle against the Sandinistas, do it on patriotic grounds. We must not forget that the members of the Political Directorate were actively involved in the struggle against Somoza. We believe that one or two persons do not present an obstacle to a unification. It is necessary, because only unity will give us the strength to win. When we began the struggle against Somoza, victory became possible only when we united our forces. And, even more important, only that unity guaranteed us international support. This is also true today.

The Washington Post, Newsweek, *and* The Miami Herald *have proven that the founding of the FDN would not have been possible at all without financing from the United States. Dollar injections were needed for building the training camps, securing the weapons, logistics, recruiting people—in short, for everything. Comandante Pastora receives money from the same sources. Isn't it true that the current arrangements with the FDN mean securing North American financing for the commandos who operate out of Costa Rica?*

We have assured everyone again and again that we don't receive any money from the CIA, but from other sources, even from individuals in Germany, Spain, Italy, and Venezuela.

But what interest is a German or Italian private individual supposed to have in supporting your movement? The history of the FDN shows that it is destined to fulfill its role in a covert war of the U.S., and that it is advised, armed, and led by the CIA and that it doesn't take money from just anywhere.

I can only say to you that you can sometimes be surprised. There are people who really have a great feeling for democracy and will therefore do everything for it. And when they have enough money, then it is nothing for them to contribute their share to the struggle for democracy.

FDN-ARDE supports the now-allied troops, as you call them. Approximately how many men are there?

I guess that we have about 16,000 soldiers, if we take the FDN, the ARDE, and the troops of Comandante Edén Pastora together. Only I do not think that the alliance brings us any nearer to the U.S. Most of the people here are unbelievably prejudiced against the U.S. and its money. No one cares what the Russians or the Cubans give the Sandinista Liberation Front. Along with that, nice little sums come from bank robberies or kidnappings, while the money that we get is clean.

We don't want to argue now about where the FSLN gets its money from. But it certainly doesn't get it from the sources you just named. The weapons that the Cubans sent for the last offensive against Somoza came much too late and weren't deployed at all but stayed in the hands of well-known Costa Rican politicians, from whom you are now buying them. The military goal of the ARDE and the FDN has for some time been the conquest of a particular area of Nicaragua, in order to declare it a "liberated territory" and install a "provisional government." The occupation of the small harbor city, San Juan del Norte, at the mouth of the Río San Juan, must be understood in this context although it is clear that this place does not have the least strategic significance and that the ARDE troops can't hold it very long. Up to now the ARDE troops have not succeeded in holding an area for any length of time.

The war we are waging is not a war of position but a guerrilla war. To defend a piece of liberated territory, we need a well equipped army. But I can assure you that there are several liber-ated areas where the Sandinista troops do not dare to go. There, the ARDE troops are in control. In the North, there is also a stretch

162

of territory where the Sandinista troops cannot penetrate. So we can say that there are indeed liberated areas, but no provisional government has been declared yet.

Until three months ago, Pastora was the military chief of the ARDE. Now he has been driven out by Fernando Chamorro. Isn't that like a small coup in your own ranks?

I wouldn't call it a coup because the military high command was abandoned by Pastora. After the retreat of Edén Pastora, the Revolutionary Directorate of the ARDE named Comandante Chamorro as the military Supreme Commander of the ARDE. Comandante Pastora is surrounded by a certain aura, but Comandante Chamorro also has a long revolutionary practice. On Nov. 15, 1962, he stormed and took a command point of the National Guard in Jinotepe and Diriamba, in the area of Carazo, with a guerrilla troop; he was a decided opponent of Somoza from his earliest youth.

Let us assume that Pastora returns to the ARDE. What would happen then in the military high command? Both appear to lay claim to being the leader.

That would certainly be worked out. We wish that Comandante Pastora would return to the ARDE. We expressly emphasized that in the communique that we put out after Pastora's separation from the ARDE. We said, word for word, that the door is always open to Comandante Pastora. I don't believe our biggest problem is how we determine the military high command if Pastora returns to the ARDE. Two Supreme Commanders could be named or we will seek another solution. What is certain is that there would be an understanding between Pastora and Chamorro. We are fighting for Nicaragua, not for personal power. Therefore I think that the two would come to some arrangement on the question of military leadership.

One of your main demands is a "general amnesty." What do you understand by that?

We demand an amnesty in the political sense, not for common criminals. We are of the opinion that there can be peace in Nicaragua only when the Nicaraguans are reconciled. We are prepared for that, at any rate, without resentment and without hatred. If we wanted to return to Nicaragua to wreak vengeance, then we would fall into a vicious circle of hate, murder, and crime. The Somoza supporters must also have the right to return to Nicaragua. If they have committed a crime, then they must be handed over to the courts. Only in this way will there be peace in Nicaragua again.

That is probably a lot more difficult than you would like to think. What about someone like Juan Zavala, who functions now as adviser to the Chamorro ARDE movement? He was involved in a million-dollar gold smuggling scheme and was only able to get refuge in Costa Rica through a cloak-and-dagger action. And what would you do with the ARDE soldiers and officers who killed a lot of people, such as, for example, the ARDE soldier who threw a hand grenade into a hole in a resettlement village near San Carlos, although he knew that women and children were hidden there? Should a general amnesty include such people?

Yes, but as I said, we are concerned with the political cases first. For them there must be a general amnesty.

The UDN-FARN, a part of the ARDE, had plans to blow up a refinery, a cement factory, and other strategic installations. Terrorist actions and sabotage always endanger the civilian population, and to an even greater extent when they are planned actions [attacks on major installations].

In our military strategy we have never planned violent acts of this type. I say that, although I have no military responsibility. The oil tanks bombed in the harbor of Corinto are beyond the residential section. But you can't always prevent the killing of civilians in war. Purely terrorist acts, however, like exploding a bomb in a place where only civilians can be hurt, should be condemned.

But it always comes down to terrorist acts by your side. More than once, for example, the leader of a cooperative has had his family murdered before his eyes. Or hit lists are compiled of those to be systematically eliminated.

I know of no such hit lists. Perhaps with the FDN, but not with us. People die in this war, but in battle. We had about 220 prisoners. About half of them stayed with us. We handed the rest over to the Red Cross. That is really a humane gesture. Indeed, we know that the majority of the people who fight in the ranks of the Sandinistas are forced to do so, for different reasons. Some for economic reasons, because they can't earn a living any place else, and others because their families live in Nicaragua and they fear reprisals against their families.

The rainy season has already begun in Nicaragua. Military operations are possible now only under the most difficult circumstances. However, since elections take place in November, the ARDE announced a military offensive for September. What is the meaning of that, what is the goal?

You know that one characteristic of guerrilla war is that there are always stages of gathering your strength and of going on the offensive. We find ourselves now in a stage of gathering strength in order to begin an offensive in September. The FDN also announced an offensive, and we agree with them. There is a coordination between the military leadership of the FDN and the ARDE.

Do you have a common strategy, will you go forward together?

We do not want to change our previous strategy because our situation hasn't changed. Right now we are in a difficult situation. There is a flood of farmers who want to fight on our side, so great that we can't even accept them all.

Why not, aren't there enough weapons?

We don't have enough weapons, we don't have enough money.

And the FDN has enough?

No, I don't think that exactly...

FDN weapons or arms which are lost or broken are replaced by the Americans. The FDN has lost airplanes and helicopters. An ARDE helicopter was confiscated by the Costa Rican Civil Guard not long ago and after a few weeks it had disappeared, like magic. One source of conflict between Pastora and Robelo is a helicopter that Robelo is supposed to have swiped.

I would have to pass there, I don't know anything about that. I have political responsibilities, I don't know anything about the military area.

What is the now-unified movement called?

It doesn't have a name yet. Perhaps directorate or alliance, if we come to an alliance with the FDN within the framework of a democratic, national reconciliation. We haven't found a name yet. We have begun talks with MISURA, which operates in the North under the leadership of Steadman Fagoth, and we have already united to coordinate military operations. We have also made progress in political coordination.

Does that mean that MISURASATA, under the leadership of Brooklin Rivera, doesn't work with you?

Indeed, MISURASATA, which is led by Brooklin Rivera, does not work with us.

Then with whom?

With Pastora.

If an alliance with Brooklin Rivera is not possible, why should there be an alliance with Fagoth?

I believe that we will all close ranks more and more. Unfortunately, Brooklin has left the ARDE. We are now making progress according to our great plan of rapprochement and alliance with the FDN, and in this connection we will deal with MISURA as well. And I am sure that, unified, we will one day move into Nicaragua. Brooklin will not be able to stand back.

And Mr. Dávila, who has connections with the Christian Democrats, is also on Pastora's side?

Dávila doesn't represent the Democratic Christian Solidarity Front. What he says is his personal opinion.

Up to a week ago you could read something else about Dávila and ARDE.

True. He was the representative of the Democratic Christian Solidarity Front until Pastora left. Then he took Pastora's side and our organization decided to relieve him of his post, following an election and an internal reorganization. Today our General Secretary is Dr. Roberto Ferrey, and Aníbal Ibarra is a member of the ARDE directorate. José Dávila now speaks only in his own name.

Fernando Chamorro is now Supreme Commander of the ARDE troops. And the FDN also has a Supreme Commander.

A position claimed by Pastora.

If we unify the FDN, then certainly the military side would have to be thought through anew. Then there could be only one Supreme Commander, one Comandante General, one General Staff, or whatever you want to call it. But that shouldn't really create a problem. There are agreements, on both sides here, about naming one person as the military leader.

Edén Pastora says all the time that he wants nothing to do with former National Guardsmen. But ex-National Guardsmen were instructors and also troop leaders in the ARDE. Doesn't that make the politics of this alliance difficult?

We do not allow former members of the National Guard who

were the closest allies of Somoza and who committed crimes against the Nicaraguan people to participate in our struggle. But the National Guardsmen who have a clean slate can fight with us perfectly well. We have always said that, and Comandante Pastora himself has had people from the National Guard in his ranks.

And there is still one interesting phenomenon: the ARDE troops of Comandante Pastora have already made contact with the troops of the FDN. There is already coordination and mutual assistance between them. They are in contact in the Bluefields area, and in Nueva Guinea, deep in the interior. In Chontales as well.

Are you claiming that Pastora can no longer resist "the Guard that murders the people," as he once called them?

It is difficult to uphold such an opinion in practice. It is difficult because you can't forbid a person who is fighting from making contact. I think that this process of rapprochement is a question which will be answered in the course of the struggle. And the most important factor is that, at this base level, the beginnings are there. Then the leadership must follow, because otherwise there is a break between the leadership and the base.

"In Ocotal,
All Hell Broke Loose"

Conversation with
José Aquiliano Sarmiento Martínez
and Mauricio Sánchez García

First of all, tell us your names, how old you are, and where you come from.

I am José Aquiliano Sarmiento Martínez. I am 18 years old and was born on October 4, 1966, in El Limón de Pucayá in the district of Ocotal.

And you?

My name is Mauricio Sánchez García. I am 23. I was born in the valley of La Paz. This is part of Totogalpa, in the district of Somoto.

We would very much like to know how you were recruited by the FDN.

José: On March 7, 1984, we went to spend the afternoon in a valley near the village of Antigua with a small group of friends. It was the day some of us had been marked with the sign of the cross on our foreheads after Mass. We were sitting under a tree, talking about all kinds of things, when we were suddenly set upon by a group of armed men. We later learned that they were part of a combat group led by "El Griego," the Greek.

They came from Honduras and were headed toward Pueblo Nuevo, so they had to pass through our valley. "Here's the find we've been looking for," said one of them, who came from the same area as me. He knew that my brother was fighting with the Sandinistas, and that I worked in the village cooperative and also with the CDS.

Then and there, they took me and two others with them to Pueblo Nuevo. I admit that I had a chance to take off several times, but in spite of this I continued on with them. It was more fun than going back to my family. "Stick with us," they said, "we need people. We want to fight for our fatherland, for a truly free fatherland. The people who are now in power will get theirs; you can be sure that we will win."

It's true that once they've snatched you up, you feel a little of their power yourself. That makes an impression. This is what happened with me. I really felt stimulated. Yes, and I went along with them, without any training, without having any real belief in it. We didn't get far on the first day, only to a small farm they knew of, where we spent the night. I had the feeling that they were watching us.

The next day we got as far as the asphalt road to Pueblo Nuevo. There was a skirmish, and they took two more farm boys with them. On the first day they had already given me an AK, as a sign of trust, because two of their group had taken off and left their weapons behind. I now had a machine gun and 170 rounds of ammunition. In this first battle, in Martillo, we got hit pretty badly. The fellows from the Sandinista army pumped us full of lead. We pulled back around 5 p.m. I was still wearing the same things I'd worn on our walk. My left shoulder hurt a little from the AK strap hanging on it. They encouraged me and said I would become a good fighter.

What about you? Were you two already together at that point?

Mauricio: No, not yet. When José joined, I was already in the La Lodosa camp on the Honduran side. I was sick, with a high fever. All my bones ached. It rained constantly the whole time, and it was damned cold.

I finally got into a clinic, where all the wounded who came over from Nicaragua were treated. They told me I had malaria, gave me a couple of shots, and kept me there a few days.

When I was on my feet again, we really had to work hard. We had to gather wood for the whole camp and build latrines. We did everything ourselves in the camp. We were also trained during that time.

At home, I had always done everything myself, too. I grew the rice, beans, and corn. I worked as a day laborer for anyone who offered me work. When things got tight again, I told my mother I was going to work as a coffee picker at the La Providencia ranch, near Quilalí. I had to earn some money because I no longer had any shoes. That was in February.

I arrived Sunday and started picking coffee on Monday. I can still remember the day, February 16. In the middle of the night there was suddenly a loud noise at the door. I was half-asleep as I heard, ''Get up! If you don't, we'll fire a round into you.'' There were only a few people in the house, four, I think—the others were away. Armed men stormed the door and pulled us from our beds. They ordered us to come with them at once and dragged us outside.

Around midnight we were taken to some empty houses. They gave us sugar cane to chew on, so we wouldn't be hungry.

At daybreak we had to get up and march with them until the sun was high in the sky, through mountainous terrain the whole time, along the Honduran border. At a certain point we crossed the border into Honduras.

We finally came to a village called Las Dificultades. The troops who tried to get new men from Nicaragua came from that village. I think they went from ranch to ranch to recruit or draft people.

It was about noon when we arrived, and right away we got something to eat, beans and cooked bananas. Afterward, we could lie down. I think I slept until the next morning. The next day, I saw that the group was growing—more and more civilians were coming from Nicaragua. Soon we went farther, to the camp at

La Lodosa. About 40 peasants had been brought from Nicaragua. We were allowed to rest for three days, then came the training.

And you, José, were you also taken along to Honduras?

José: Yes, we were taken directly to Honduras. On Wednesday we took the asphalt road toward Pueblo Nuevo.

Why do you remember it was Wednesday?

José: Well, I've got a good memory. I know that we stayed in Nicaragua exactly 22 days before we pulled back into Honduras. That was on a Wednesday. They grabbed me on a Wednesday, and it was on a Wednesday that we crossed the asphalt road.

Then we entered a village called La Jagua. They told us, "From here we are going down into the valley, in order to cross the Panamerican at Ocotal during the night. Then we'll be at the border by morning." There were 20 of us. They had taken most of us by force. They always told us they had too few people—enough weapons, but not enough people. It's clear that they took along anyone they captured.

We arrived in Honduras the same night and arrived at La Lodosa camp early in the morning.

How did you know that it was Honduras?

José: They told us that right away. After we had crossed the border, they said, "Now we're home. There is no more danger. Here we are in Honduras, our brother country."

How was the camp set up?

José: Nothing special, except for a sick bay where those who had been wounded in the fighting were patched up again. Next to this was a storage area for corn and beans, and the camp kitchen, where all the cooking was done, mostly noodles, beans, corn cakes. There were women who did the cooking there. A man made the coffee. The weapons store was well-stocked: FALs, AKs, and also RPG-7s, as these weapons are called. The weapons were also cleaned and stored there.

What went on during a normal day at La Lodosa?

José: There was constant movement in the camp, with people going back and forth all day. Trucks loaded with boxes usually arrived at night, and we would have to get up at 1 a.m. to unload them. We had to get up at 4 a.m. every morning anyway. Everything had to be done quickly because we were still being trained.

They really lit a fire under us to keep us going! During the first days at the camp, we didn't have to do anything. We could bathe and only had to gather a little wood. This was only true for the five of us who were the youngest. The youngest was 15, the others 17, and I was just 18. We were able to rest for three days. Then came the Comandante, "Mac." Comandante "Mac" is a tall, sturdy black man with a heavy nose, while "Z2" is small and fat and has long, curly hair. "Mac" held the reins in the camp, and also gave orders to the "El Griego" combat unit and other combat units. "Z2" is a deputy and also sort of a bodyguard. When "Mac" isn't there, "Z2" always stays in the camp. In La Lodosa camp there were three "trainers": "X7"; "Cuadrito," the Cadre; and "Calladito," the Quiet One.

When I was in the camp, "X7" and "Cuadrito" were not there. Comandante "Mac" turned us over to "Calladito" with the order, "Here are the new boys, you won't have any trouble with them." On the first day of training, he taught us how an FAL is dismantled. After that we trained with AKs and M-14s. I had never held a weapon before. Later the physical exercises began. Up and down, up and down the road, so we became more nimble and learned to control our bodies. We also learned how to keep hidden but still move forward. This whole process lasted eight days. Then "Calladito" said, "So, that's that. You are now trained. That's enough."

All in all, the training lasted more than a month. We had to dig holes, build latrines, reinforce the roads. The camp is located in a very sandy area, and the trucks often got stuck up to their axles. After the training was over, we marched back into Nicaragua.

Comandante "El Griego" had left his entire combat unit under the command of "Samuel" in Nicaragua, and came back to Honduras with "Ocre" and "Panter." They were both "El Griego's" bodyguards. They came to get us up: "Get ready, we're going over," ordered "El Griego." We put on uniforms and new boots and packed extra uniforms and boots to take with us, because his men didn't have boots and clothes. We crossed the border near Mojones. There were about 20 in the group, including Mauricio. Together with the other commandos, there were 60 of us.

We stayed a month on the Nicaraguan side until the Sandinistas attacked us from a mountain. It was the first battle of my life. For the first time I really fought. We began to pull back but immediately ran into our next battle. As we took up our position, Comandante "El Griego" said to us: "We're going back to Honduras tomorrow and you'll go back with us." For 22 more days we moved through the region, before we returned to Honduras.

What did you do during those days?

José: We didn't do anything. We rested in our hiding place or were ordered to recruit people. But no one from this area wanted to come. Then we returned to Honduran territory.

We crossed the main road near San Fernando, in the vicinity of Ocotal, where we fell into a trap. The Sandinistas had fortified themselves in the mountains and attacked us as we crossed the road. I was already in my third battle. We suffered casualties in this battle. Since we had no time to bury the dead, we just left them behind.

We always tried to take the wounded with us so they wouldn't fall into the hands of the Sandinistas. I saw how they buried one man called Rudolfo. We did not speak about the dead. We told no one about them, not the family, no one.

Were you together at this time?

Mauricio: When we crossed the border with the clothes and the boots we were together. I came back to Honduras with "El Griego's" battle unit.

There were 215 men who went to recuperate in La Lodosa camp. I was sick, still had malaria in my bones, and needed treatment by a doctor.

Ten days later, Comandante "Mac" arrived with "Z2," "Calladito," the others. They conferred all morning and then in the afternoon gave the order to move out. We were to be on the road to Jalapa for four days. We were a pretty big combat unit. Two other units were added.

We marched into Nicaragua to a village called Ojo de Agua. We slept in a clearing that the woodcutters had made and waited until Comandante "Mac" came. He brought along "Delfino" and some women. I can still remember one named "Little Dove." She was, I think, "Mac's" secretary. The other was called Carmen María. She was a nurse. "Mac" and "El Griego" always withdrew completely for their discussions, so that no one could overhear them. They decided that "El Griego's" combat unit would march on and "Ocre's" would remain. I was in "Ocre's" combat unit and was armed with an FAL. My AK was given to one of the women. We continued on—along cattle trails.

At about 5 p.m. we came to a bare plateau. There we met a couple of people who were taking a break from their work. They took us to their homes in the nearby village of Jaragua.

From there we went on. We even had to march at night. No one was allowed to remain behind. Since we were not used to night marches, we were soon worn out. But if someone couldn't go any further they lit a fire under his behind. I carried 500 rounds on my back, which weighed about 25 kilograms. In addition I had a couple of RPG7 hand grenades. You had to be as strong as a mule to stick it out.

Around 4 a.m. we arrived in the vicinity of the city of Ocotal.

We didn't see "El Griego," who was already far ahead of us with his two women, "La Mula" and "La Lombriz."

What did you do when you returned to Honduras the second time?

José: We only stayed a short time in Honduras. "El Griego" said to us, "In a few days we'll return to Nicaragua." "That's fine," said the group leader, who was in command, "we'll stay here and rest up."

We spent the time close to the border, on a hill. Some read the Bible and the others chased women. In every camp there are women. I washed my uniform and bathed several times. All day long, mules arrived loaded with provisions. We cooked our meals ourselves. Later the mules came just to bring ammunition, M-79 grenades, RPG7s, and mines.

One evening we were told that the next day we would be going back to Nicaragua, because there were lots of troop movements there. We were allowed to eat one more big meal and were given a small ration of dry food for four days. The rations were in packets—one packet per day. I carried an M-14 and 600 rounds of ammunition. Eight M-79 grenades and real Claymore mines were distributed to one group. The others had exclusively FAL weapons. We all wore the blue uniform. This uniform is very good, though it sometimes falls apart at the shoulders. It's really good in the rain, and lasts a long time.

Another day Comandante "Mac" and "Z2" gave speeches. I didn't get much out of it because I was standing quite far from them. "Mac" said in general that our victory was still far in the future, that it would be more than just a few days.

At midday [on the march to Nicaragua] we marched on. All together there were about 445 of us. The next day we reached Ojo de Agua, where we split up. Our group went on alone, along secret paths that no one else knew about, close to the border. You had to be really careful because the Sandinistas had mined the paths and also laid mines in the hills. Comandante "Ocre" went ahead of us with his group. I heard a kind of muffled bang and thought it was a bomb. It was a mine, and two men were badly hurt. As I passed the place, all I could see was how everything had been sprayed with blood. I saw nothing more of the two men. I don't know if they were wounded or killed.

On Friday at 11 a.m., in Ojo de Agua, someone said to me, "Here comes our Master." It was Comandante "Mac," who brought a pack of pamphlets for us to leave behind along the road. The commanders then sat down together to prepare for the next advance. When everything was clear, "Mac," "Ocre", and "El Griego" synchronized their watches. It was 12:30. They gave the order to march. Our guides were peasants from Mozonte. They were cattle herders and knew all the secret paths and hiding places.

When we arrived in Jaragua Valley it was already early Saturday. We still didn't know what we were going to do and still didn't know our goal. One of us, a man named Pijul, suddenly said, "Good grief, I bet I know where we're going. We're going to Ocotal." "La Mula," who was standing nearby, was very amused and suggested that if we seized Ocotal, we could really get ourselves decked out. It was still a long way to Ocotal. The day had not yet dawned. Somewhere dogs were starting to bark. At the turnoff to Ocotal, "El Griego" said, "This is where we will meet again, after the assault, right here at this spot."

Everyone suddenly started whispering. No one was supposed to know that a group was passing by. We turned right and went down from the road and up the other side of the steep bank of the river. Behind me I heard a deep sigh from "El Malo." "I've gotten this far—this is where I'm going to stay." "That's fine," said "El Griego," "I'll march ahead with 'El Pescado,' 'La Mula,' and 'Gitano.'" I stayed with "El Malo's" combat group. I had eight M-79 grenades and Claymore mines. At times Daniel helped me carry them.

It wasn't long before we heard the first shots. We couldn't figure out where they were coming from, and Daniel told me to fire at the small hill in front of me. Maybe the Sandinistas were there. Nothing more came at us, and we were told that a lot of fighting was going on in the city. From the city we could hear "El Griego" saying over his megaphone, "Long live the FDN." But as far as we could see, they got no support from the inhabitants. They fought alone in the streets.

I waited a while longer and suddenly two boys came by carrying "El Griego." He had been shot through both legs. "Yes, I got hit," was all he said. Suddenly we were in the middle of a bombardment by the Sandinistas. We were at about the first intersection outside Ocotal, still on the edge of the city. The others [Sandinistas] were on the other side—they could easily control the junction. We hadn't thought that the Sandinistas might pursue "El Griego" and block the line of retreat for all our troops. Many fell as they tried to retreat. Real chaos broke out. We were being shot at from all sides and fled down the river bed close to Ocotal. I saw "El Pescado" clear out with his people. I never saw Daniel again. "La Mula," our leader, paid no more attention to us. We had no idea what to do. We simply stopped moving.

Suddenly we heard a sharp voice cry, "I think there are 10 of those blue shitheads back there." And then, "Surrender!" I pulled myself together, jumped up and ran across the river bed. I had the damnedest luck, because just at that moment a grenade went off. I threw myself down, but then above me I heard a helicopter, very low, and the others were bellowing, "Get away, just get away. That idiot thing is about to lay an egg down here." I stumbled blindly behind them. We knew nothing about what happened to "El Griego"—if he was dead or if the Sandinistas had taken him with them. We ran until we were totally exhausted. When we couldn't go any further, we hid ourselves in some brush. "El Pescado" was nearby with his people. He took command and said, "We must make sure we get out of here." As we pulled ourselves together to take off, we were fired on once again by the Sandinistas. Suddenly I realized we were surrounded.

Still we ran on. "El Pescado" ran ahead and we followed. Suddenly I felt an electric shock in my leg, and I felt very warm. I immediately threw away everything I still carried—my weapons and my backpack, the grenades, and my beautiful knife, which I had taken from a dead man. It's too bad, that knife was really beautiful, with inlay on the handle.

When I really couldn't go any further, I asked "El Pescado" to help me. But he only called back to me, "If I help you, I'm done for myself." I could go no further and lay with my face in the dirt. It was over, the end, I simply couldn't go on. Suddenly I was incredibly afraid and thought, now it's really over with. Soon you'll be done for. Then the Sandinistas arrived, combing the whole terrain. "Look at this one," they said, "this one even my grandmother would give away."

They hauled me up on the bank and asked me a bunch of questions. They wanted to know about the attack on Ocotal—whether we were trying to capture Ocotal or only attack it. I told them that of course we were trying to capture it. They thought that was crazy, since the Sandinistas were so completely in control. Even if we could have captured Ocotal, we certainly wouldn't have been able to hold it. They took me to their leader, who arranged for someone to wash out my wounds. Then they took me immediately to the Ocotal hospital—later to the military hospital in Managua.

Does your family know what happened to you?

José: No, they know nothing about it. I believe they think I'm dead. Since March 7, I've had no more news of my family. They haven't shown any signs of life. I don't even know if they are still alive. The whole family lives in El Limón. We're a large family—nine brothers and sisters. I am the youngest. One of my brothers is fighting with the Sandinistas in Ocotal. The others are involved in farming. They all work in the fields, just like I used to, and they all live in my parents' house. With the new cooperative we had already begun to cultivate corn, beans, and coffee. There's enough land there to make a living on. We'd gotten far enough to get a team of oxen.

Mauricio, were you also at the attack on Ocotal?

Mauricio: Yes. We got as far as the river bed. We were the middle group. I really don't know how we could have succeeded in this attack. We were totally exhausted when we stormed Ocotal. I remember that at the first crossroads, I leaned against the wall of a house to rest a little.

We passed Rafael's group on the way to Zompopo. He marched with his people to Ocotal. Over the megaphones they yelled, "Viva el FDN," and "With God and patriotism, we'll defeat Communism." I passed someone—I still can't believe it—taking pictures in the middle of all this. He was a foreigner, who joined us.

I took shelter because I had never been in a fight before. I had no idea what was happening. I was afraid. "Man, get going! Go ahead, shoot!" Nothing. I did nothing. I pressed myself against the wall, and it was like I was numb. I only hoped that it would all be over soon. One of the women came by and shouted at me, "Son of a bitch, you're shitting in your pants! Look at me. I'm a woman and I'm not afraid!" The woman stormed down the street and continued to yell, "Damned shithead! A man has to fight at the front and not press himself against the wall." She simply went on ahead. Her name was Xiomara, and she was unbelievably brave. She returned once more. "Give me the FAL. Mine isn't working anymore—it's jammed somehow." I didn't want to give it to her, but she tore it out of my hands, stood in front of me with her legs planted far apart, and screamed, "But the magazine is still full, you haven't fired a single shot! My five magazines are empty, and I have already shot some out of the other one!"

We ran on down the street together. Then I saw how they had pulled down the red and black Sandinista flag from the radio station and set it on fire. The whole time, we were being shot at. "El Griego" was hit by a full blast. A medical orderly tried to reach him, but he got a direct hit near his heart. Once again I hid against the wall, completely rigid. Next to me someone my own age fell to the ground like a sack, shot in the head. Then everyone ran back past me, and I ran after them. I jumped down a little slope, and as I jumped I suddenly felt a muffled blow in my hip area. I felt paralyzed, and was barely able to rip off my backpack. I fell down next to a mango tree. Someone else was already lying there. His name was Miguel. I knew him from before. He said to me, "Now you've had it, too. You won't get out of here. Put a bullet in your head, so you can't tell them anything. Watch me." I couldn't take it in. He bent toward me, put the FAL in his mouth, under his tongue, and pulled the trigger. I saw how his head was ripped backwards and his brains spattered against the tree trunk. That was Miguel. He must have been about 35 years old. About eight meters away lay another one. He had a stomach wound. He had seen what happened and called over to me, "I won't let the Sandinistas cut my head off, either. Before that, I'll kill myself." He set his weapon on automatic and shot the whole magazine into his own head.

I was totally wiped out and had already lost a lot of blood, when one of the Sandinistas called over, "Now, my little friend, put your hands up high or we'll blow you to pieces." I didn't have a weapon anymore. When they saw I was unarmed, they came over to me and asked if I could still walk. Then two of them put their hands under me and slowly brought me down the slope to the street. Two more joined them, and they put me on their shoulders. They carried me right through the city.

They wanted to know a few things, but they quickly saw that I was too far gone. They put me on a pickup truck and took me to the hospital. The doctors there worked on me, gave me a few shots and pills, and a drink. In the Ocotal military hospital they operated on me. Then they took me by ambulance from Ocotal to a military hospital in Managua. I had never been in Managua and I had never dreamed that I would see the capital city for the first time from an ambulance. Until then I'd only been to Totogalpa and Ocotal, where we'd go when we had to buy things, but that was very seldom.

Do you have family? Do you know what's happening with them?

Mauricio: I still have two sisters and three brothers. The youngest is 13. My father doesn't have his own land—he's a farm hand. My grandfather, however, had a piece of land that belonged to him alone. When he died, he left his land to an uncle who lived in Asunción. One day my father simply cleared out. I was about eight years old then. He found a job with the post office in Matagalpa and he never came back. All of us remained with my mother. She worked in the fields and we helped her, but we still had to work for other people, too, so we'd have enough to eat.

When the contras took me with them, at first I really felt bad. Twice I ran away and twice they caught me. They threatened to kill me if I tried to escape again. So I stayed, but I never really came to terms with them. I was always sad when I thought of my family and how they were feeling without me. They certainly suffered because of it. You see, they knew nothing about where I was.

Did you believe what the contras told you about the Sandinistas?

Mauricio: I wasn't sure. I have often seen the Sandinista army. I knew the battalions. Many times they marched by our house and stopped for a rest under the big tree in front of the house. I heard them talking with pride about how many contras they had shot. They were amazed that the FDN simply left all their dead behind and often their wounded as well.

Comandante "Mac" once said to us, "There is only victory— you must believe in it. If you doubt, you'll fall flat on your face without even noticing it." He asked us if things were going well at home, if anything had changed, if things were going better for us since the communists had been in power.

I can still remember how pissed off he got when people gave some examples of what was good in Nicaragua. "Shits! Snotnoses!" he'd say. "You just don't get what's really happening in Nicaragua. There is no soap, there is no toilet paper. I think it's about time that we finally lit a fire under the Sandinistas' rear ends."

Why did you join the FDN?

José: Not because the Sandinistas were after me. I believe I didn't really consider it carefully. I mostly worked at home and things weren't going so badly for me. I actually trusted in the Frente (FSLN). There were about 50 of us fellows in the valley who wanted to organize a cooperative. We got weapons in order to defend ourselves and PROCAMPO [Programas Campesinos]. But that was just at the beginning, and we still had lots of problems. Since then the whole valley has probably organized itself.

Comandante "Calimán" marched through the valley with his group and took some of the young men with him. About seven months ago "Calimán" suddenly stood in our doorway, pointed at me, and took me with him. In the four neighboring houses he did the same thing. I was able to escape that same night, along with my brother. We sneaked out through a small window. Today I still don't know how we did it. We ran like the devil. "Calimán" was really a pig. Once I saw how he went after a Sandinista. He just wasted him. That's what he did with peasants if he found out that they were working with the Frente. He simply knocked them in a heap, without wasting any time, just "bam." After that, I saw "Calimán" in the La Lodosa camp. He was a horror. Small and secretive as the devil. He was a specialist in bank robbery.

Can you tell us something more about the camp? Were there also Hondurans there?

José: The Hondurans had their border post not far from us. They called us "The Green Ones." From time to time they came by to get medical supplies from us. But once four men, Hondurans, came by from the FDN General Staff and made a couple of speeches to us. One was dressed in civilian clothes and spoke in a language I didn't understand. He wore thick glasses and was pretty strong. I think he spoke English.

Do you know what's happened to the other boys from your neighborhood?

José: We were split up. One was in "La Mula's" troop, the other with Rudolfo. He was killed pretty quickly down in Magdalena Valley. The other one from our neighborhood went to JMI, which had almost no people left. They were all dead or wounded, which is why he was sent to that group.

Couldn't the people who came from one particular area stay together?

José: No, I don't think so. At any rate, we were all split up, put in different groups. Naturally I would have preferred to stay with my brother or with my cousin. But we were sent to different camps right away, with people we didn't know.

Did you get a wage?

José: No, we didn't get one córdoba, just food. And that was only when there was some. There were days when there was nothing, and then of course we didn't eat anything.

"The Gringos Know How To Do Things"
Conversation with "Pecos Bill"

Why are you lying here in the Danlí Hospital in Honduras? Do you have gunshot wounds?

No, I was not wounded in the war. I must have a gastric ulcer or something like that, which has been troubling me for months.

When did you leave Nicaragua?

I was a lieutenant in the National Guard, so of course I had to run away on July 19, 1979.

What did you do then?

I immediately looked around to see what could be done. In 1980, in Guatemala, I belonged to the FRENICA, then to the Legion of September 15th, and when the FDN was founded, to the FDN. From the beginning I was with the contras. Even when there were different organizations, they were really only different names for the same thing. First it was the FRENICA, the Revolutionary Nicaraguan Front, then the Legion of September 15th, and then the FDN—it's all the same, always the same people, but always better armed with more and more money.

In your opinion, how will the struggle end?

I believe we will win the war as long as they all continue to support us strongly. If they do not give us enough support, we will have to keep operating as guerrillas. Then we can throw away the modern weapons, because there will not be any more ammunition. We will have to grab the AKs of the Sandinistas, and fight like the Vietnamese in Vietnam did. Naturally we will win the war much more easily and faster if the U.S. keeps on supporting us. But if they don't want to do it anymore, there are other ways to continue the fight. Let's hope that good old Mr. Reagan will be re-elected—then we will get all the stuff we need, and also enough bucks.

How were the Sandinistas able to overthrow Somoza?

The Sandinistas talked in foreign countries everywhere about how they would be democratic, which is what people wanted to hear. They blinded the people, cheated them. They were able to overthrow Somoza because he was a symbol of dictatorship. But Somoza—I'm not so sure, I was only a lieutenant—Somoza was not that bad. The vultures around him were beyond any dignity, a bunch of pigs. They fooled the people and made them believe that Somoza was—excuse the expression—a turkey stuffed with shit. The fact is, the Sandinistas had planned beforehand to set up a Marxist-Leninist government. And look at it today! Now there really is a military dictatorship in Nicaragua! They are nothing but lackeys of the Cubans, and the Cubans are—excuse me—the Russians' ass wipers.

What is the relationship of the Honduran government to the FDN? What can you tell us about this as an officer?

We stay out of their business and they stay out of ours. We stay here on the border and do our job. They always drive around a little bit to see if everything is OK. Otherwise we have nothing to do with each other. If they need us for anything, then we give them all our support, but except for the transportation of our equipment and our supplies they leave us alone. Our position is clear: the Honduran government is helping us, therefore we don't cheat them.

Have you felt any changes since General Alvarez was replaced by General López as Secretary of Defense?

Yes. After that, a lot happened. Before that, it was like in Vietnam: three fourths of our forces were in reserve and one fourth in Nicaragua. General López made it so that we put our activists more and more in Nicaragua. We used Honduras just as a point of departure. Now we have nearly all our camps along the border. We can't go to Tegucigalpa as often to get drunk and to feel under women's skirts. But that's OK, because shit like that has cost our group a lot of money, which we certainly could use for better things. I agree with having some forces in reserve, but there were too many who strolled around and too few who fought. A fight is the best education. If you see that your rear end is about to be fired at, then you pull yourself together and see what needs to be done.

Were there more attacks recently?

Now we operate inside Nicaragua—at least 85 to 90% of our troops. So we are steadily taking more and more territory, despite the fact that the Sandinistas are also using newer and better tactics. They mine the border and use more artillery. But actually they are on the defensive; they have already lost the offensive. They don't go in the jungle to look for us because they know what would happen to them. They only defend their positions.

But the guerrilla warfare battalions, the BLI, also roam the thickest jungle?

Yes, those are their special units. You have to hand it to them—they're an equal opponent.

What do you do if a BLI team is behind you?

We try to waste them, of course. They are only drilled by Cubans, but we at least have an ideal that strengthens and motivates us. We want Nicaragua to be a democracy again. That gives us enormous strength. The Sandinistas are only paid soldiers. We are volunteers. None of us gets paid.

How was the FDN built?

After July 19, some of us escaped to Guatemala. Francisco

Urcuyo—he was the last Nicaraguan President, Somoza appointed him before his retreat to Miami—had gathered a small group around him, about 45 people, who founded the FRENICA. There were other small groups also. They were all coordinated and trained by a Cuban exile from Miami. One fine day this Cuban-shit disappeared with all our money—it was a pretty good amount—and he was not seen again. The individual groups joined together and founded the Legion of September 15th. The first small training camps began in Honduras. In the beginning, we had only sticks instead of guns for training. Later, Argentinian teachers arrived, really good people. We got our first guns then. I went to Costa Rica for awhile. When I returned I practically fell over, seeing the many good new things that were there. FAL, M-50, M-60, grenade throwers, all the stuff you need for fireworks. I believe the FDN is better armed than the Honduran army. Our fighting morale is also better than that of the Hondurans. When they see Sandinistas, they shit in their pants and run like some-body had put a chili up their ass.

Why did you go to Costa Rica?

In Costa Rica, I worked for some time for the Salvadoran secu-rity service. But it's better if I don't talk any more about that. The result was that I was expelled. Maybe you remember: In 1982 a Salvadoran diplomat was expelled from Costa Rica. The newspapers naturally did not write about me, but I was also there.

Tell us again what happened to the Salvadoran diplomat.

There were six Cubans who tried to smuggle guns and ammu-nition over to the Salvadoran guerrillas. We put a bomb in their car, but it didn't go off right. It did explode but none of them was wasted. We also arranged some fireworks inside the Rus-sian embassy at San José, with a fourth of a stick of dynamite. The Russians gave a big party, and I was ordered to finish it off pretty clean. I went there and finished it off. I didn't transfer any-body to heaven, but that wasn't what I was ordered to do. They told me to end the party, so I did.

Do you know Edén Pastora personally?

No. When I was in Costa Rica, they asked me if I wanted to fight with his movement, the FRS. But first I wanted to know more about it, so I had several meetings with FRS people. I quickly realized that they are also Sandinistas, and they still can't stand National Guardsmen. They're crazy, they believe they could move forward in this struggle without the support of the U.S. In general, they talk a lot of shit about the U.S., about the FDN, and about the National Guard, and in fact about everything. I think Edén Pastora is not a real democrat. He is some kind of a socialist, with a left-leaning tendency. I don't think it would be a good thing if Pastora got to power in Nicaragua. Then I would fight my own battle against him. But if we are going to win, then we must all get together: MISURA, FDN, and also ARDE. Pastora continually talks about how he wants to have nothing to do with the FDN, that we're all Guard. The FDN is 95% peasants and probably 3 to 5% National Guard.

But they have the power to command, or . . . ?

Sure, we know our business.

What do the military plans of the FDN look like?

The camps in Honduras, which until now have been decentralized, will be replaced by a large camp, Banco Grande—the point of departure for attacks inside Nicaragua.

Will there also be camps set up in Nicaragua?

We still have one camp in Zelaya, in Cantayawas. This area was freed by Comandante "Tigrillo" and his crew. We will therefore move part of our troops into this area. In Banco Grande, battle units are now forming into a new regional command, which will soon be sent into the interior of Nicaragua. The special units are already in Nicaragua. Also, at La Lodosa and Las Vegas, battle units are being centralized into a regional command to be sent to

Nicaragua with all their stuff, as quickly as possible. Then La Lodosa and Las Vegas will be joined together.

What are you doing now?

We have our own special troop, named COE-078, all Nicaraguans. We are supplied directly by the U.S., but we don't have advisers from the U.S. The Argentinians—instructors and advisers—also left about a year ago. They built up and supervised everything we did and were very satisfied with us. Now we are in the middle of the offensive, which will last some time. We have pushed the Sandinistas into a corner. There's no doubt about that.

When will the war end, in your opinion?

If we continue to get such good support, we will probably be able to finish the war by the end of the year.

There is a Russian AK standing by your bed. Where did you get it?

I don't know. I think the Israelis or the Americans sent them to us. In any event, suddenly they were here.

You are a well-trained soldier. Did you get your training only in Nicaragua?

No, in the U.S., too. I was sent there as a very young guy, to the Valley Forge Military Academy in Pennsylvania. This is a private military school, which has a good name in the U.S.

The training is certainly very expensive. Who financed it? Your parents?

My parents are well-to-do ranch owners from Chinandega, rich people. They owned a big herd of cattle. They were expropriated by the Sandinistas. I don't dare think about that, because then I see red. This is what I want to pay the Sandinistas back for.

After finishing the military academy, did you return to Nicaragua?

No, I joined the U.S. Navy. I served in it for several years and learned a lot. That's why I speak such good English.

Why do you call yourself "Pecos Bill"?

That's a funny story. I'm sure you know Pecos Bill is a legendary American cowboy. When I returned from the U.S., I enrolled at the Nicaraguan Military Academy. On my first day, I wore a cowboy outfit to school. The others thought this was pretty neat. I looked like a real Texan. From that day on, I was "Pecos Bill" to everybody.

Have you also been inside the Miskito camps in Honduras?

Yes. At the beginning, I trained Miskitos for the FDN at Camp Rus Rus. The Miskitos are a lazy bunch. Most of them don't want to be anything, and only hang around. You wouldn't believe how many of them run away. They just desert after we have finally put a bit of courage into them.

How are the Miskitos recruited?

We go into the refugee camps and select candidates for the next training course. But why should the people be better than their leader, Steadman Fagoth? I think he's a little crazy. He only comes by once a month to visit the camp and otherwise he runs around. I think he lives in Tegucigalpa. That's no way to lead an army.

What do you train the Miskitos in?

Communication techniques.

Where did you learn that?

I learned the basics in Israel. I was there for six months when I was still in the National Guard. We were given a special course in how to fight guerrillas. Later I took a course in Panama, given by Americans. They trained me in the "Escuela Las Americas" for jungle war. What a great course that was! The gringos know how to do things.

Recently there were some changes within the General Council. It is even said that Comandante Echaverry, "Fierro," was elimi-

nated. Edgard Antonio Hernández, "Abel," also has not been seen for a long time, and Comandante "Suicida" may be in hiding.

"Fierro" went to Argentina, so far as I've heard, and "Abel" died of a heart attack.

Do you really believe that the FDN security service boss died of a heart attack? Weren't powder burns found in the area of his heart?

It was really time to clean up the General Council. They no longer represented our goals and they put the money in their own pockets. They strolled around in "El Bechi," the best whore-house in Tegucigalpa, and wasted money on alcohol and sex. It was a scandal. So our new General Council had to clean it up, put things in order, and force off the stage some of these people whose role was finished. "El Suicida" overplayed his cards. I believe he wanted to start his own army. So he was liquidated.

GLOSSARY

This listing has been prepared for the U.S. edition.

Organizational Acronyms

ARDE. Alianza Revolucionaria Democrática (Democratic Revolutionary Alliance). Costa Rican-based contra organization.

CDS. Comités de Defensa Sandinista (Sandinista Defense Committees). Nicaragua's largest mass (civilian) organization.

EEBI. Infantry Basic Training School. Elite counterinsurgency force headed by the son of Anastasio Somoza.

FDN. Fuerza Democrática Nicaragüense (Nicaraguan Democratic Force). Honduran-based contra organization.

FRENICA. Frente Revolucionario Nicaragüense (Nicaraguan Revolutionary Front). Contra organization from earlier period.

FSLN. Frente Sandinista de Liberación Nacional (Sandinista National Liberation Front). Leading force in the struggle against Somoza; official party in power in Nicaragua since the 1984 election.

MISURA. Name represents the Miskito, Sumu, and Rama indigenous peoples of Nicaragua. Contra organization.

MISURASATA. Name represents "Miskitos, Sumus, Ramas, Sandinistas Working Together." Organization originally established by the revolutionary government of Nicaragua, then taken over by contras.

UDN. Unión Democrática Nicaragüense (Nicaraguan Democratic Union). Contra organization, later became part of ARDE.

Code Names of Contra Personages

"Abel." Edgard Antonio Hernández
"B-1." Jorge Ramírez Zelaya
"El Fierro." Emilio Echaverry (Echevarri)
"El Judío." Emerson Iriel Navarrete
"El Muerto." Pedro Núñez Cabezas
"El Negro." Fernando Chamorro
"El Policía." Armando López
"El Suicida." Pedro Pablo Ortiz Centeno
"Renato." José Francisco Ruiz Castellanos

ABOUT THE AUTHORS

Dieter Eich, born in 1946, is a native of Germany. He holds a Ph.D. in sociology and is a specialist in military history. He has authored various publications on the state and the military in Latin America. As a sociologist and an engineer by profession, he has worked in Ecuador, Peru, and Spain, and currently heads the office of the West German government's Development Agency (DED) in Nicaragua.

Carlos Rincón, Ph.D., is a Colombian and was born in 1940. Dr. Rincón is a noted scholar in literature and Germanic studies, and served for many years with UNESCO in Vienna. His published works include over 20 books on such topics as changing conceptions of literature, Latin American theory and criticism, and the Enlightenment in Spain, Portugal, and Latin America.